D1080088

Twentieth-Century Scotland

TWENTIETH-CENTURY SCOTLAND

A Pictorial Chronicle 1900 – 2000

Edited by Martin Hannan and Donald MacLeod

MAINSTREAM
PUBLISHING

EDINBURGH AND LONDON

First published in Great Britain in 2000 by
MAINSTREAM PUBLISHING COMPANY (EDINBURGH) LTD
7 Albany Street
Edinburgh EH1 3UG

ISBN 1 84018 308 X

A catalogue record for this book is available from the British Library

Typeset in Sabon
Printed and bound in Great Britain by Butler and Tanner Ltd

INTRODUCTION

At the end of the most momentous century in human history, Scotsman Publications have joined with Mainstream Publishing to mark 100 years of Scottish life. This pictorial history uses the archives of Scotsman Publications, who have been at the centre of Scottish life throughout the century, to create a record of a changing Scotland and a changing world. No single book could attempt to be a comprehensive record of the whole century, and we make no claims to detail every facet of Scottish life. Instead, *Twentieth-Century Scotland* provides extended snapshots of the main events that shaped the century, and charts the development of elements of Scottish life such as culture and the arts where the true picture only emerged over a longer period.

We would like to thank the tireless and ever-patient staff of the library and photographic archive departments of Scotsman Publications for their invaluable assistance; Cathy Mineards and all the staff at Mainstream Publishing for their coffee and co-operation; Janene Reid for her design; and principally Alan Taylor and the management of Scotsman Publications for their support of this project.

Chief credit, however, must go to the many photographers and reporters whose work is included in these pages. They have created a chronicle of an amazing century and in doing so have themselves made history. Apologies are made in advance for any omissions, which will be rectified in the next volume – which we hope you will be around to purchase in 2099.

Martin Hannan and Donald MacLeod
December 1999

REPORTAGE

Some of the most vivid memories we share are those of events which touch a chord in us all – the accidents and disasters which cause sudden and heavy loss of life. Often these events can be recalled by just one or two words – Ibrox, Lockerbie, Piper Alpha, Dunblane. In the twentieth century, Scotland has been the scene of some of Britain's worst disasters, and the reports of them, especially those of more recent times, still have the power to unsettle us. This section chronicles the reportage of those disasters which occurred in and around Scotland or which featured Scots.

5 April 1902

The first Ibrox disaster

On Saturday, 5 April 1902, almost 80,000 people crowded into Ibrox Park, Glasgow, to witness the Scotland v. England international. There had been overcrowding and confusion before the game but nothing to indicate the forthcoming tragedy. *The Scotsman*'s account was as follows: 'The game had not long been in progress when, shortly before four o'clock, a portion of the terracing, packed with a seething crowd of humanity, gave way under the unwonted pressure, and between two and three hundred of the spectators were precipitated to the ground from a height of forty or fifty feet.'

Fans flooded on to the pitch to escape the panic, though such was the crush that many in the same terracing had no idea what had happened. The authorities, fearing a riot, allowed play to continue after 15 minutes.

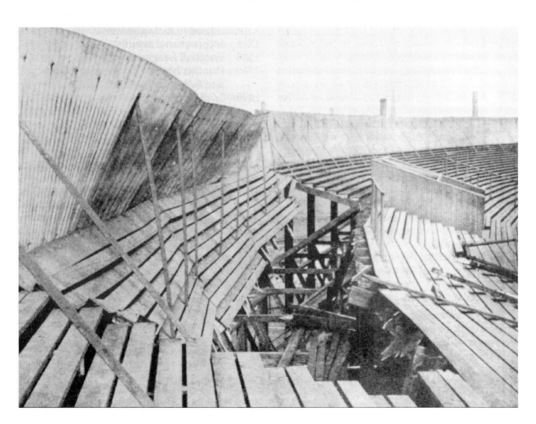

In all, some 25 people died, with a further 537 people being injured. One of the consequences of the tragedy was the abandonment of wooden terraces and the building of largely stone and brick stadia such as the rebuilt Ibrox, Celtic Park and Hampden.

The wooden terracing which collapsed at Ibrox, killing 25 spectators

9 May 1911

Empire Theatre fire, Edinburgh

Sigismund Neuberger would never have made it in showbusiness if he had not changed his name to The Great Lafayette. In 1911, the 40-year-old American was the world's greatest illusionist, travelling with a small orchestra and a real lion. He was booked for a short season at the Empire, now the Festival Theatre, when a personal tragedy struck him on 6 May. His beloved dog Beauty, a gift to him from Harry Houdini, died and was buried in Piershill Cemetery in the capital. Lafayette ordered that wherever he died, he was to be cremated and his ashes buried back in Piershill with Beauty.

The show had to go on, and on 9 May the 'house full' signs were out at the theatre in Nicolson Street. The last illusion by Lafayette was just coming to an end when an arc light or paper lantern fell and started a blaze which quickly spread through the entire backstage area. The safety curtain could not be lowered fully, and although the audience escaped, the cast and backstage crew were in great peril. The Great Lafayette had ordered doors to be locked to protect his secrets, and although *The Scotsman* reported that the illusionist was seen 'doing his best for the members of his company', he and nine others were unable to escape. The dead included 17-year-old Alice Dale, who played the charming 'teddy bear' in one illusion, and the lion.

Burned beyond recognition, Lafayette's body was eventually identified by his rings. After a funeral in which thousands lined Princes Street, his ashes were interred alongside Beauty in Piershill Cemetery, where they lie to this day.

The Great Lafayette and Beauty

14 April 1912

Titanic sinks

On her maiden voyage, the Belfast-built *Titanic*, pride of the White Star Line and claimed to be unsinkable, hit an iceberg in the Atlantic and went down with the loss of 1,600 lives. Among the passengers and crew were many Scots, including First Officer William Murdoch.

In common with most newspapers, *The Scotsman* first reported that all the crew and passengers were safe; these reports were based on an erroneous message flashed from New York. In those early days of radio and telephone communications, such mistakes were common, although in the *Titanic*'s case there was a suspicion that the false message had been given to allow insurance companies the time to disperse their risk and cut their losses. However, there was no doubting the import of a message which

made the following editions of the paper: 'Steamer *Olympic* reports steamer *Carpathia* reached the *Titanic*'s position at daybreak, but found boats and wreckage only. She reports *Titanic* foundered at about 2.20 a.m. in latitude 41.16, longitude 50.14. All the *Titanic*'s boats are accounted for. About 675 souls saved of the crew and passengers. The latter nearly all women and children.'

More than 80 years later, the film *Titanic* sparked a row in Scotland when the valiant First Officer William Murdoch of Dalbeattie was depicted shooting passengers and then himself, when in fact he had been one of the crew who had stayed aboard to ensure passengers' safety. The film-makers had to apologise to the townspeople, for whom Murdoch remains a hero.

Top: First Officer William Murdoch

Above: The telegram which reported the disaster to the world

Titanic leaving port on her maiden voyage

The trains burned for hours
after the crash

22 May 1915

Gretna rail disaster.

It was, reported *The Scotsman*, 'a disaster unparalleled in the history of British railways'. On a bright May morning, a signalling error on the main west-coast line caused a train carrying troops mostly from the 1/7th Royal Scots to strike a local passenger train and both were derailed at the Quintinshill siding a mile north of Gretna. About three minutes later, as the injured milled around, a northbound London to Glasgow express ploughed at almost full speed into the derailed trains and another train on an adjacent siding.

The aftermath of the disaster

Fire broke out and engulfed the scene. Frantic rescue efforts by soldiers and local people were largely defeated by the blaze, during which gas cylinders exploded regularly. In all, 226 people died, 214 of them soldiers. Mercifully, most had died instantaneously during the first and second collisions, although some burned to death as their colleagues fought in vain to save them. Afterwards, steps were taken to ensure that gas and other inflammable materials on trains were stored away from passenger areas. Such a combination of crash and fuel-filled fire did not occur again until the Paddington disaster in London in October 1999.

In 1915, *The Scotsman* reported bleakly: 'The disaster is of a character and magnitude unexampled in this country.' To this day, the loss of life in the crash remains the largest in any British rail disaster.

1 January 1919

The sinking of the *Iolaire* off Stornoway

On Hogmanay 1918, the former yacht HMS *Iolaire* set out from Kyle of Lochalsh for Lewis, bringing home some 250 servicemen who were desperate to reach the island for Ne'erday and the traditional celebrations. For some it was the first time they had been at home to bring in the New Year since the outbreak of war.

The Scotsman reported on what happened shortly after 2 a.m. on the morning of 1 January 1919: 'As the vessel drew near to Stornoway, for some unaccountable reason the *Iolaire*, instead of entering the harbour, ran right across its mouth, and struck the rockbound shore at the reef significantly named the Beasts of Holm.

'Buffeted by the wind, the ship was turned broadside on, and lies submerged between the Beasts and the shore from which she was only a few yards distant.'

Some 60 men had jumped into the water at the point of impact because they could see land just yards away, but the *Iolaire* dragged them down with her. Others got into the two inadequate lifeboats which were swamped, drowning a further 40. In all, 205 men lost their lives, nearly all of them from Lewis. Crowds gathered on the shore to await the mostly tragic news that their relatives had survived a world war only to die in sight of home.

The Scotsman noted: 'Hardened as the nation may have become during the past four years to death and destruction on an unprecedented scale, people cannot read the story of the Stornoway disaster in its pathetic circumstances without a feeling of peculiar poignancy and sympathy.'

The *Iolaire* in her previous incarnation as a naval yacht

The ship submerged off the Beasts of Holm

31 December 1929

The Glen Cinema fire, Paisley

The worst cinema fire in British history caused the largest peacetime death toll from a fire on the Scottish mainland. It was the age of the victims and the almost pathetic nature of their death as well as the scale of the tragedy which caused all Scotland to mourn at Hogmanay 1929.

A Western had been showing in the packed Glen Cinema when a reel of film started to smoulder. It was thrown out of the projection room and the thick smoke started a panic among the 600 children in the auditorium. They dashed for the rear fire exits away from the smoke but toppled over each other in the stairway, causing a crush which suffocated those at the door, which was in any case barred and prevented exit. The fire itself petered out when the manager threw the burning reel outside.

Firemen had already arrived and had dashed inside without smoke helmets, such was their concern for the children. The damage had already been done, however, and all day and into the night the sad sight of parents arriving to identify their dead children haunted the Royal Alexandra Infirmary. None of the 69 young victims had burn injuries. The New Year of 1930 was brought in not with cheering, but with tears for the dead children.

RUSH IN PANIC ON ALARM OF FIRE.

MASS OF STRUGGLING CHILDREN ON STEPS TO CLOSED EXIT.

TRAMPLED DOWN BY TERROR-STRICKEN COMPANIONS.

THE greatest disaster in the annals of the British cinema industry occurred in Paisley yesterday afternoon, when sixty-nine children were killed and many injured.

The children were attending a special "Hogmanay" matinee performance in the Glen Cinema, where a frantic struggle for life followed a panic.

The panic was caused by the ignition of a film, which, having caught fire, was thrown out of the operating box.

Late information confirmed the fact that the fire was confined to the film from the operating box, and that most of the children lost their lives through suffocation from fumes in the rush to escape.

Conflicting reports of the death-toll were current, and it was only after some time that the victims could be identified. Nurses were overcome at the spectacle of the apparently unending procession of dead children being carried into the hospital mortuary chapel.

Great heroism was displayed by a number of policemen and civilians in attempting and effecting rescues.

A special meeting was called by the Provost of Paisley last night, and a letter of sympathy was issued to the townspeople.

"It had been my intention," wrote the Lord Provost, "to send a New Year greeting to you, to convey my good wishes for a happy and prosperous

10 December 1937

The Castlecary rail disaster

An unnamed *Scotsman* reporter found himself the unwitting observer of Scotland's worst peacetime rail disaster of the century in which 35 people were killed at Castlecary in Dunbartonshire. The Edinburgh to Glasgow express ploughed at full speed into the rear of another express running from Dundee to Glasgow which had stopped because of the heavy snow blocking the line.

The correspondent wrote: 'The scene was reminiscent of a clearing station for the wounded in France during the war. The only difference was the fact that women and even children were among the victims. Many of them were crying but still displayed courage, as women with young children declined to be treated until their youngsters had received attention. The fortitude of these women was a feature of a terrible experience.'

HEAVY DEATH-ROLL IN SCOTS RAILWAY DISASTER

Edinburgh-Glasgow Express Crashes Into Stationary Train

24 KNOWN DEAD; 18 BODIES SO FAR IDENTIFIED

Others Still Under Wreckage; Search for Victims Throughout Night

RESCUE WORKERS TOIL IN RAGING SNOWSTORM

10 January 1947

Explosion and fire at Burngrange Colliery

The Midlothian pit of Burngrange was rocked by an explosion and a fire which brought mine rescue and the emergency services rushing to the colliery. Despite their heroic efforts, a total of 15 men died in the disaster. An inquiry found that the explosion was caused by the use of acetylene lamps. Modifications were ordered to the design of such lamps – but, as so often happened in pit tragedies, the improvements in safety came only after the loss of life.

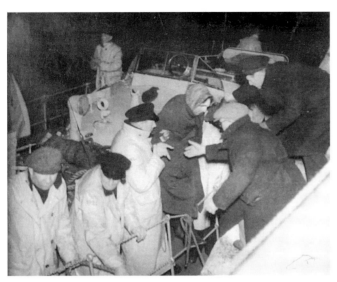

Passengers being helped ashore after their rescue

31 January 1953

The sinking of the *Princess Victoria*

A hurricane during which the winds were measured at 110 mph swept over Scotland and on into the Netherlands and Belgium in the last weekend of January 1950. More than 200 people died on the Continent, many when the Dutch dyke system was overwhelmed, but the biggest single loss of life came with the sinking of the *Princess Victoria*, a ferry on the Stranraer to Larne run.

The ship, built by Denny's at Dumbarton, was just five years old when the storm claimed her early into her morning run to Larne. The exact sequence of events was never known, as her skipper, James Ferguson, was one of those drowned. Inspections showed that her sea doors had been smashed in by the ferocity of the gale-lashed waves and her car deck had flooded, causing the eventual capsize. Confusion surrounded the SOS signals sent by the ship as she had been blown many miles off course and was near the Irish coast when found. *The Scotsman* reported one rescuer saying: 'We just didn't know at the crucial time exactly where we should go.'

A total of 133 passengers and crew perished. The owners, British Railways, were later reprimanded following extensive inquiries into the sinking, which was Scotland's worst post-war shipping disaster.

An aerial shot of a lifeboat being towed to safety

18 September 1959

Auchengeich Colliery disaster, Chryston, Lanarkshire

Scotland's worst mining disaster of the century hit Auchengeich pit in the early morning when miners were returning to work after a three-day strike. A 'bogey' train carrying 48 miners deep underground ran into a fire believed to have been started by an electrical short circuit. The train retreated before the deadly fumes hit but one man, Tommy Green of Glenboig, feared they were going too slowly and jumped out to run ahead of the train. He was the only one to survive. After futile rescue efforts the pit was deliberately flooded to put out the fire. *The Scotsman* printed the tragic death roll which showed that the 47 victims came from a triangle bound by Kirkintilloch to the north, Shettleston in Glasgow and the Chryston area of Lanarkshire.

A scene all too common in Scotland's pits in the last 100 years

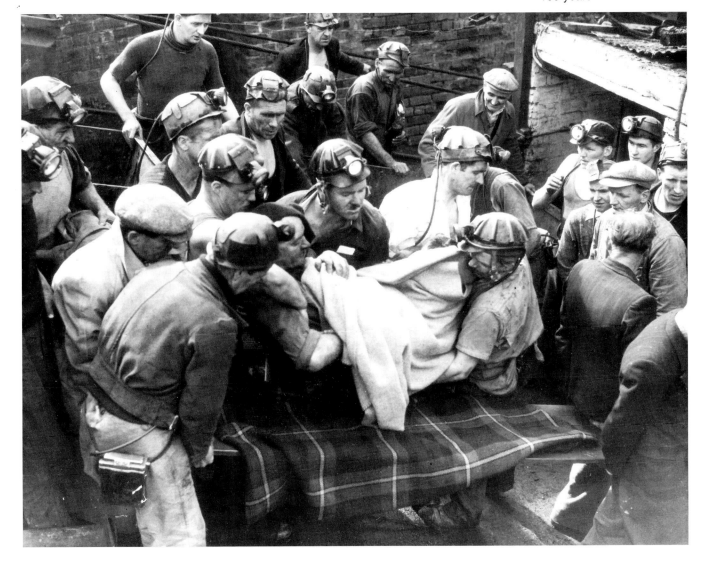

NINETEEN DIE IN GLASGOW WHISKEY BOND INFERNO

Collapsing wall buries two fire-engine crews and five salvage workers

FLAMES LEAP-FROG NARROW STREET TO SECOND WAREHOUSE

28 March 1960

Cheapside bond fire, Glasgow

Glasgow's fire service had battled many blazes over the years alongside the city's unique Salvage Corps. Both services had been called to a whisky bond in Cheapside Street just yards from the River Clyde when an enormous explosion blew down a 60-foot-high wall, killing 14 firefighters and five salvage workers.

The Scotsman reported: 'The flames, which could be seen two miles away, were so intense they leap-frogged the street to another whisky bond, setting it on fire.'

Unprecedented scenes of mourning followed the fire, with Glasgow paying due tribute to the fire service it so often called upon.

January 1968

The great hurricane

On 15 January 1968, Scotland was hit by a hurricane in which the winds often reached 100 mph and more. The results were devastating. More than 1,000 homes were destroyed, there was extensive structural damage, especially in Glasgow, people were killed in their homes and on city streets by collapsing masonry, and others were killed in their cars by falling trees. In all, some 21 people died in the hurricane.

Later that year, on 18 November, 22 workers in an upholstery warehouse in James Watt Street perished when they were unable to escape fumes and flames. Many of the dead were found piled behind a locked fire exit.

HUNDREDS HURT OR LEFT HOMELESS

120 m.p.h. gusts wreck houses and cars

Nineteen people died in Scotland yesterday when gales that roared up to 124 miles-an-hour smashed their way across the country leaving a trail of shattered houses, crippled ships and wrecked cars. The screaming wind that battered homes and gave most of Scotland a sleepless night was the worst in living memory.

21 January 1970

Fraserburgh lifeboat loss

On a stormy day in the North Sea, a year after the loss of the Longhope lifeboat with all hands, the Fraserburgh lifeboat overturned when hit by a freak wave while escorting a Danish fishing ship into harbour. Only one man survived. It was the third loss of the Fraserburgh lifeboat this century, two of the crew having drowned in 1919 and six having been lost in February 1953, the same year in which the Arbroath lifeboat sank with the loss of six crew members. The Broughty Ferry lifeboat also lost crew in 1959, and the memorials to these and other losses remind us of the high price that volunteer lifeboat sailors have often paid for their courage.

The actual moment of the lifeboat's sinking – its stern can be seen to the right of the mast of the fishing boat

Below: So many people owe their lives to the bravery of the crews of the RNLI

2 January 1971

The second Ibrox disaster

Stairway 13 at Ibrox had been the scene of the death of two people from crushing when a barrier collapsed in 1961 and was just a few yards from the scene of the first Ibrox disaster in 1902. Despite a portent of the tragedy to come when 24 people were injured in 1969, no one could have predicted the awful sequence of events during the traditional Ne'erday game between Rangers and Celtic.

With 80,000 people in the ground to witness what many recall as a very sporting clash between the old rivals, Celtic scored late in the game, causing many Rangers fans to leave. But an equaliser in the dying seconds caused some to turn back or halt on the stairway and an irresistible crush built up, causing steel barriers to twist like balsa wood. An unknown person was seen to fall and within seconds bodies went down like ninepins, piling two metres high with those underneath being crushed and suffocated to death. Many fans left the ground not knowing that their fellow spectators were dead or dying. A massive rescue operation swung into operation but it was too late for 66 people, the

Stairway 13 shortly after
the crush

youngest of whom was just eight.

More than 100 people were rushed to hospital and some were left disabled by their injuries. The Fife village of Markinch lost five schoolboys in the disaster, which directly led to the reconstruction of Ibrox.

The Scotsman's John Rafferty, the finest sportswriter of his day, turned news reporter to record his impressions: 'I had taken to the match a Brazilian sports journalist. The sporting spirit of the match was not what he had been led to expect. We left the stadium and he said "nothing happened". I tried to explain that there was much myth about Rangers–Celtic matches. We went down Copland Road and there was the screech of a racing police car and then another with blue roof-light flashing. We went into the ground. There were many passing us with that strange look on their faces that comes with terror. Clearly there was horror near and then it was at our feet in a misshapen childish body, muddied and bloodied.'

Differences between the Old Firm were set aside as Scotland mourned the dead of the country's worst sports-related disaster. Many involved that day were scarred for life both physically and mentally. Former captain John Greig, who was playing for Rangers that afternoon and is now the club's PR executive, recently told *The Scotsman*: 'I have been involved with Rangers for around 35 years and, irrespective of everything I have been through, that is the saddest day I can remember.'

Later that year, the Clarkston gas explosion devastated a pristine new shopping centre at Clarkston on the south side of Glasgow. It was only after heavy cranes were brought in to lift huge chunks of concrete that the final death toll of 20, with 105 people injured, was established.

Jock Wallace, the man who later led Rangers to European triumph, helped to carry away the injured

The dead lay covered in tarpaulins until they were moved to a makeshift morgue

6 November 1986

The Chinook helicopter crash, Shetland

Apart from the Lockerbie bombing, Scotland's worst civilian air disaster took place off Sumburgh Airport, Shetland, when a giant Chinook helicopter of British International Helicopters crashed into the sea while bringing ashore oil workers from the Brent field. Only two of the 47 people on board survived the crash, the cause of which is still disputed, though an official inquiry blamed a fault in the gear wheel of the twin-bladed helicopter.

Crash: 45 feared dead
Chinooks grounded afer worst helicopter tradgedy

By DAVID STEWART and SIMON BAIN

All North Sea helicopter flights using the Boeing Chinook were suspended last night, after the worst signal, and none of the lifejackets on the survivors or on the dead had been inflated. The survival suit those chartered by Shell, a fourth Chinook is on charter to Britoil.

Mr Ian Henderson, Shell

6 July 1988

Piper Alpha

Scotland's worst industrial disaster and the world's worst oil-rig fire happened at night while many men on the rig were asleep. A small escape of gas caused an explosion which in turn triggered a fireball and further explosions which engulfed the Piper Alpha oil rig operated by Occidental Petroleum. There were 226 men on board Piper Alpha when it exploded. The speed of the spread of the fire trapped some men in their accommodation while others died trying to use escape hatches and boats.

Within 30 minutes, the rig was effectively consumed by fire. Flames shot 500 feet into the night air as a massive rescue operation began. Many of the 62 initial survivors – one died later in hospital – escaped by leaping into the sea from more than 130 feet up.

Others managed to get down to a lower level using ladders and ropes before jumping off. Once in the water, they had to face blazing oil on the surface which hampered rescue attempts. Two rescue workers also died, giving a final death toll of 167, with 30 bodies never found.

Many of the men who survived had horrific burns injuries and a large number of them would not return to work on the rigs, so traumatic had been their experiences. Texan oil-rig firefighter Red Adair was called in to assist in the process of finally extinguishing the blaze almost two weeks after it had begun. The remains of Piper Alpha were later sent to the bottom of the sea.

Piper Alpha ablaze shortly after the explosion

Opposite: Piper Alpha's ruined hulk burned for days afterwards

21 December 1988

The Lockerbie bombing

Scotland's worst peacetime disaster occurred just after 7 p.m. on 21 December 1988 when a bomb blew apart the Boeing 747 of Pan Am flight 103 at almost 34,000 feet above Lockerbie.

A total of 259 people who were bound for New York from Frankfurt died in the catastrophic descent. *The Scotsman*'s reporter on the scene found 60 of their bodies lying on the local golf course. In the fireball on the ground, 11 Lockerbie people were also killed. The townspeople earned themselves a worldwide reputation for quiet dignity in the awful aftermath of the disaster.

The dead came from 21 nations and their ages ranged from two months to 82 years. For many years it seemed that they would have no justice, that no one would ever stand trial for their deaths. Parents and relatives of the dead, however, notably Dr Jim Swire, led the long campaign for the truth to be established.

Led by Scottish detectives, police made inquiries in 70 countries and took 15,000 statements. Some 18,000 items of property were retrieved and recorded and 35,000 photographs were taken. Charges were laid late in 1991 against two alleged Libyan intelligence agents, Abdelbaset Ali Mohmed al-Megrahi and Al Amin Khalifa Fhimah. Libyan leader Colonel Gaddafi refused to allow their arrest and sanctions were imposed in 1992, including bans on air travel and sales to Libya of weapons and certain types of oil-related equipment. In addition, Libya's financial assets abroad were frozen.

In 1999, after 15 months of intense but patient diplomacy by the British, US and Dutch governments, the two accused were handed over to stand trial at Camp Zeist, now officially Scottish soil, in the Netherlands. United Nations Secretary General Kofi Annan, South African President Nelson Mandela and senior Arab leaders had all assisted in the negotiation. The law of Scotland has been altered to allow the trial to take place overseas in front of a bench of judges rather than a jury. The prosecution's contention that the bomb was put in an unaccompanied case at Malta and transferred on to flight 103 at Frankfurt has frequently been challenged in the last eight years. The trial should begin early in 2000 and could last a year or more. No matter the outcome, it is already set to be the trial of the next century.

The largest piece of wreckage was half of the first-class cabin and aircrew deck

A giant scar was ripped through Lockerbie

The *Braer* being torn apart
on the rocks

5 January 1993

The Braer disaster

Scotland's worst oil spill came not from an oil rig or pipeline as many had feared
but from an ageing Liberian-registered tanker, the *Braer*, which ran aground in
fierce gales on Shetland, spilling its cargo of 85,000 tons of light crude oil into
some of Scotland's most unspoilt waters.

The ship's engines failed and she was swept ashore, the 34-strong crew being
winched off by coastguards and the RAF. A massive pollution-containment operation swung into action, but it looked likely that it would fail as oil leaked into
the sea to form a seven-mile-long slick. Indeed, the Ultramar company, owners of
the cargo, later had to stump up millions of pounds to compensate Shetlanders
for the loss of their salmon fisheries, for polluted land and even for sheep which
had been contaminated by the oil spray.

Her cargo despoiled fish,
animals, birds . . .

. . . and crops alike

2 June 1994

Chinook crash, Mull of Kintyre

In an accident which had major ramifications for the Northern Ireland conflict, an RAF Chinook helicopter flew at almost full speed in a mist into the coastal hills of the Mull of Kintyre while on a secret flight to Fort George near Inverness. All 29 people on board the helicopter perished in the crash and resultant fire. They included 25 of the province's top counter-terrorist experts, including members of the intelligence services, and high-ranking army and police officers. An RAF inquiry blamed pilot error but press investigations and a Fatal Accident Inquiry cast doubt on this explanation.

Mystery still surrounds the crash of this Chinook . . .

. . . which left this horrific aftermath

13 March 1996

The Dunblane massacre

No event in recent Scottish history has caused more horror and revulsion than the massacre of 16 schoolchildren and their teacher in the quiet town of Dunblane in March 1996. On the morning of 13 March, Thomas Watt Hamilton, a loner with a grudge against a society which allowed him gun licences but had deprived him of access to young children in 'boys' clubs' which he ran, walked into Dunblane Primary School armed with four powerful handguns.

This is how *The Scotsman* reported the event the following day: 'He walked past classrooms, crossed the dining room and went to the assembly hall where 29 children aged between four and six were having PE exercise under the supervision of Gwen Mayor, 44. At 9.28 a.m. Hamilton opened fire in the school and within two minutes 15 Primary 1 children and Mrs Mayor were dead. Two other teachers and 12 children – one of whom died later – were wounded. Another adult was also injured, but was later discharged from hospital. Hamilton, 43, of Kent Road, Stirling, then turned the gun on himself.

'At 9.38 a.m., Central Scotland Police control room received the first report of a "firearms incident" at the school. A full tactical operation, including officers with guns, was initiated. At 9.46 a.m., the first police officers arrived to find what Chief Constable William Wilson described as a "scene of carnage". Local doctors and crash teams from hospitals in Stirling, Falkirk and Glasgow rushed to the school to help the wounded. Within minutes, ambulances and a helicopter were ferrying the wounded to hospitals.

'News of the incident swept through the close-knit Perthshire town and by 10.30 hundreds of parents and relatives had flocked to the school gates. Between 10.30 and 11.30, police commandeered a restaurant beside the school where relatives could shelter. They were then taken into the school in batches of ten where their names were checked with the school roll and the early list of the dead and

Parents rushed to and from the school

Comfort was freely given

wounded. For the next several hours stunned parents, their emotions swinging between intense relief and distress, trickled through the school gates clutching the children who had escaped the carnage.'

The horrific events put Dunblane in the world's headlines. The press descended on the town, though most left a few days later when asked to do so by the relatives. The day after the massacre, Ian Bell captured the mood of Scotland when he wrote in *The Scotsman*: 'For what it's worth, I can tell you that this one, small nation, dressing its children for school, preparing for another hard day, and suddenly afraid for everything it cares about, directs all the hopeless love it has towards a small town in Perthshire. The defective species, eloquent beyond its own understanding, calls that humanity.'

In the days and months that followed, it seemed as if the world reached out to Dunblane. A unique outpouring of grief and sympathy led to a massive fundraising campaign which eventually raised several million pounds for the families and the town of Dunblane.

A public inquiry disclosed that Hamilton had been allowed to keep his gun licences despite the misgivings of some police officers. Led by some of the parents, an ultimately successful campaign was launched to ban handguns throughout Britain.

Gwen Mayor and her class

ROYALTY

No other element of the British state has been subject to such constant public scrutiny as the monarchy and the royal family. For most of the century the media's coverage of their activities was largely reverential, but in recent years we have learned much more about the inner workings of the 'firm', as the Duke of Edinburgh once named it, and not everything that has been revealed has been edifying. The royal family has also moved with the times, and it is worthwhile considering that the painful modernisation of the monarchy would have been anathema to the British political establishment and the public of the early part of the century.

The monarchy has also survived major constitutional crises, namely the abdication of Edward VIII in 1936 and the long marital difficulties and eventual divorce of the present Prince of Wales and Princess Diana. Due to her worldwide fame, the latter's tragic death in 1997 was the most high-profile event to affect the royal family in the modern era, but at various times during the century Britain saw both mass outpourings of grief to mark the death of royalty and great celebrations to welcome their births and marriages.

4 August 1900

Her life has spanned the century and she has been the most famous Scottish woman of the past 100 years, but when Elizabeth Bowes-Lyon, later Queen and Queen Mother, was born into one of Scotland's oldest and noblest families, it happened in England, though the exact location has been disputed.

A few months later, on 22 January 1901, the death of Queen Victoria at the age of 81 brought an end to an era named after her. The longest-living and longest-reigning British monarch had ascended to the throne at just 18, and she presided over an age in which Britain reached the zenith of its power and influence.

Lady Elizabeth Bowes-Lyon

Glasgow grocery magnate Sir Thomas Lipton's yacht on which Edward VII nearly perished

Edward VII, his son George V to his right and his grandson Edward VIII to his left

22 May 1901

The new King, Edward VII, escaped drowning when the British contender for the America's Cup, the racing yacht *Shamrock II*, was badly damaged off the Isle of Wight. The yacht was owned by the Glasgow grocery magnate Sir Thomas Lipton.

6 May 1910

A bout of pneumonia worsened rapidly and after just a few days' illness King Edward VII died, shortly before midnight on 6 May, to be succeeded by George V. *The Scotsman* reported on the crowd outside Buckingham Palace hearing the news: 'At about twenty minutes to one, a clergyman was seen approaching from one of the entrances to the Palace. In a low voice, so low as to be heard by only those around him, the clergyman announced that the King was dead. Hats were at once removed and the crowd stood in reverent silence.' His funeral two weeks later was attended by seven kings and more than 50 princes, princesses and dukes.

The Duke of York, later George VI, with his fiancée, Lady Elizabeth Bowes-Lyon

26 April 1923

After a nervous courtship in which she at first refused his proposal, Lady Elizabeth Bowes-Lyon married the Duke of York at Westminster Abbey. On 21 April 1926, Queen Elizabeth II was born at 17 Bruton Street, London, as the elder daughter of the Duke of York. On 21 August 1930, at Glamis Castle, Princess Margaret was born.

20 January 1936

Just a few months after celebrating his silver jubilee, George V died at Sandringham, aged 70. He was buried in the family vault at Windsor. His son, the Prince of Wales, became Edward VIII.

Accompanied by his brother, the Duke of York, the then Prince of Wales (left) arrives in Scotland

11 December 1936

'I have found it impossible to carry the heavy burden of responsibility and to discharge my duties as King without the help and support of the woman I love.' With these words, broadcast on radio, King Edward VIII abdicated the throne of Britain. His affair with twice-divorced American Mrs Wallis Simpson and the growing crisis over Edward's determination to marry her against the wishes of the cabinet and the teachings of the Church of England all took place in secret; only at the last moment did the public come to learn of the serious problems afflicting the monarchy. Edward's younger brother, 'shy Bertie', became King George VI, and the present Queen Mother became Queen, much to her distaste. Edward became the Duke of Windsor but Mrs Simpson was refused a royal title. On 12 May 1937, George VI was crowned in Westminster Abbey, along with his Queen. Within a month, the Duke of Windsor wed Wallis Simpson in France, where they made their home. He died in 1972 and she died in 1986. Both were reconciled to the royal family and were buried at Frogmore.

Edward and Mrs Simpson

1939–45

The King and Queen refused to leave London, even though Buckingham Palace was hit by German bombs. Despite his speech impediment, the King also made many morale-boosting speeches, and he visited many places that had been bombed. Princess Elizabeth and the King both signed up for war work. On VE day, the royal family's popularity was shown by the vast crowds which congregated outside Buckingham Palace demanding appearance after appearance by the royals on the balcony.

After the war, on 20 November 1947, Princess Elizabeth, the heir to the throne, married Lieutenant Philip Mountbatten, son of Prince Andrew of Greece, in Westminster Abbey. The day before, he had been created Prince Philip, Duke of Edinburgh. On 14 November 1948, Princess Elizabeth gave birth to her son and heir to the throne, Prince Charles Philip Arthur George. On 15 August 1950, the Princess gave birth to her second child, Princess Anne.

Left: Queen Elizabeth after launching the *Queen Elizabeth*

Below left: An informal family portrait

Below: A royal lesson about Scottish heritage

6 February 1952

After a long battle against cancer, King George VI died in his sleep at Sandringham at the age of 56. He had been a genuinely popular king, and 305,806 people paid their respects as his body lay in state in Westminster Hall. Queen Elizabeth II was on a tour of Kenya when she learned of her father's death and her accession to the throne at the age of 25. On 2 June 1953, the coronation of Queen Elizabeth II took place amidst great pageantry and popular excitement heightened by the previous day's news of the conquest of Everest by a British expedition.

'Now I can look the East End in the face' – the royal couple shortly after Buckingham Palace was hit by German bombs

The Queen and the Duke of Edinburgh's first visit to Scotland after her coronation

Princess Margaret accompanied the Queen and the Duke of Edinburgh on a visit to the Highlands

30 October 1955

After weeks of press and public clamour, Princess Margaret announced that, 'mindful of the Church's teaching that marriage is indissoluble', she would not marry the divorced war hero Group Captain Peter Townsend, a former equerry to her late father King George.

6 May 1960

Princess Margaret married photographer Antony Armstrong-Jones, later created the Earl of Snowdon. The couple were at the pinnacle of London's social set for many years.

Three generations of the royal family and its then newest member, Lord Snowdon, at the Braemar Gathering

24 February 1981

After weeks of speculation, and after a cat-and-mouse chase involving the press at Balmoral, the public learned of the engagement of Prince Charles and Lady Diana Spencer. On 29 July, more than 700 million television viewers watched the wedding of Prince Charles and Princess Diana, with a national holiday declared in Britain. The presiding Archbishop of Canterbury, Robert Runcie, described the marriage as 'the stuff of which fairy tales are made', while *The Scotsman* reported on the considerable celebrations all over Scotland.

On 21 June 1982, Prince William, second in line to the throne, was born in London at 9.03 p.m., and on 15 September 1984, Prince Henry, known universally as Harry, was born to the Prince and Princess of Wales in London.

Together in Scotland

23 July 1986

Prince Andrew married Sarah Ferguson at Westminster Abbey. The Queen gave her second son and his new wife the titles of Duke and Duchess of York.

On 19 March 1992, amid growing signs that all was not well in the marriage of the Prince and Princess of Wales, the Duke and Duchess of York announced that they were to separate. The Duchess was later pictured cavorting naked with her financial adviser, and a divorce followed soon afterwards.

On 9 December 1992, in the House of Commons, Prime Minister John Major announced the separation of the Prince and Princess of Wales. The failure of the marriage followed years of speculation and the publication of a controversial biography of the Princess which claimed she had attempted suicide. The couple said they had no plans to divorce, but following controversial television interviews in which both confessed to having extra-marital affairs they divorced in 1996. In the week of the separation, Princess Anne married Commander Timothy Laurence in a private ceremony in Crathie Church on Deeside.

A giggle . . .

. . . that coy smile . . .

. . . the object of unwanted amusement

Opposite: A family in mourning

31 August 1997

In the early hours of a quiet Sunday morning, Diana, Princess of Wales, was killed in a high-speed car crash in a Parisian underpass. Her friend Dodi Al Fayed and his chauffeur Henri Paul, later found to have been under the influence of drink and drugs, were also killed. Photographers chasing the couple's Mercedes were at first blamed for causing the crash.

The Princess's death caused shock and grief worldwide. Tributes were paid to her work for humanitarian causes, and there was criticism of the royal family for their alleged mistreatment of the Princess. There was also a backlash against the press for hounding her. Prime Minister Tony Blair set the tone for the public grieving with his declaration that Diana had been 'the people's princess'. Floral tributes at Holyrood echoed those at Kensington Palace.

On the Saturday after her death, Diana's funeral was held in Westminster Abbey, the mourning led by her former husband and her sons, and her own

Spencer family. Millions lined the route of the cortège, while the funeral was broadcast around the world on television.

On the day after the extraordinary scenes at her funeral, *Scotland on Sunday* reported: 'In Hyde Park yesterday morning as the Princess of Wales's funeral cortège passed by, the sheer rawness of their emotions came as a shock to many who had come to pay their last respects.

'It seemed that those who had spent hours patiently waiting, clutching flowers and talking to each other about the tragic events of the past week, had not truly believed that Diana was dead. It was only when the gun carriage bearing her coffin came slowly into view along South Carriage Drive that the impact hit and the grieving began.

'As the procession passed in front of her, one woman raised her camera but appeared to be too stunned to go through with taking a picture. "Oh my God, oh my God," she said, her hands dropping back to her sides.'

As yet, no one has been charged in connection with the fatal accident. A massive fund-raising appeal has raised tens of millions of pounds for a trust fund which will ensure the Princess of Wales's good work for numerous causes carries on. Even two years after her death, newspapers and magazines still carry stories about Diana on an almost daily basis.

Death's shroud

The grief poured out

The shrine

POLITICS AND THE CONSTITUTION

Given the momentous events in Scotland's political scene in the past three years which have fundamentally changed the politics and constitution of the country, it is perhaps tempting to view these developments in isolation from the political history of the century. Constitutional change, however, was on the agenda even in 1900, when home rule for Scotland was a pillar of the Liberal Party's policies. Several attempts were made to give Scotland some form of home rule throughout the century. In all there were 24 home rule bills – mostly vain attempts by MPs to raise the topic – in parliament from 1887 to the successful Act in 1998.

This brief chronicle also displays how Scotland was a leading force in the rise of the Labour movement, and how Scottish nationalism has grown in surges throughout the century. The decline of the Liberal and Conservative causes is also shown, yet it may surprise many to learn that as recently as 1955 Scotland was a thoroughly Conservative country.

27 February 1900

What we now call the Labour Party was effectively founded when three socialist groups and 65 trade unions met in London to discuss the establishment of a distinct 'Labour Group' in parliament. James Ramsay MacDonald became organising secretary of the Labour Representation Committee, and Independent Labour Party leader Keir Hardie was seen as the founding father since it was his proposals which carried the day. Both of these self-taught Scotsmen had overcome the stigma of illegitimacy and their humble origins to become leaders of the new workers' movement. Hardie died of pneumonia on 29 September 1915.

Keir Hardie

January 1906

In the previous month, Arthur Balfour, the only Scottish Secretary to become Prime Minister, had resigned with the Tories unable to maintain the government due to internal strife over the issues of trade tariffs. Sir Henry Campbell-Bannerman, son of a Lord Provost of Glasgow, had become the second successive Scottish Prime Minister, although for a different party. He called a general election in January and won a massive landslide victory for the Liberals, with the Labour Representation Committee taking 29 seats to become a real force in politics for the first time. On 7 April 1908, with his health failing, Sir Henry Campbell-Bannerman resigned as Prime Minister and he died two weeks later. Herbert Henry Asquith took over as PM.

1909–10

In April 1909, Chancellor of the Exchequer David Lloyd George proposed the 'People's Budget', introducing higher taxes on the rich and increased duties on alcohol and tobacco. A prolonged battle with the House of Lords, which rejected the budget, provoked the greatest constitutional crisis of the century on the issue of the Lords' power. The Liberals called two general elections in 1910, both ending in hung parliaments, the second being a dead heat between the Tories and the Liberals. In Scotland, the Liberals won 59 seats – the greatest number by any party in the twentieth century – and then 58 seats.

On 10 August 1911, after Asquith, backed by King George V, threatened to create enough peers to swamp all opposition, the House of Lords passed the Parliamentary Act which ensured the supremacy of the Commons. Three months later the National Insurance Act came into force, giving benefits for ill health and unemployment – the start of the Welfare State.

David Lloyd George

7 December 1916

After reversals on the western front and at home, Asquith resigned and David Lloyd George formed a coalition government in which a Glasgow businessman, the Tory leader Andrew Bonar Law, who was born in Canada of Scottish parents, became Chancellor.

On 9 June 1917, after a sea change in public and political opinion caused

Two generations of Pankhursts were jailed for their beliefs

mainly by millions of women proving their equality in the wartime workforce, the Commons voted by a large majority to give women over 30 the right to vote.

31 January 1919

Within 18 months of the Russian revolution – *The Scotsman* famously opined that Lenin and Trotsky wouldn't last – and after years of simmering industrial discontent on Clydeside including wartime strikes, the Clyde Workers' Committee led a strike calling for a 40-hour week. The strikers converged on George Square, where the Riot Act was read to them by Glasgow's Sheriff Principal. Violence flared around the city centre and the following day, for the first time in a British city, tanks were sent in to quell disturbances. The government genuinely feared the start of a British revolution and the activities of the Committee brought workers' leaders such as David Kirkwood, John Wheatley and Willie Gallacher to national prominence. The legend of Red Clydeside was born. The more Marxist approach within the Independent Labour and Communist Parties made the Red Clydesiders significantly more radical than the rest of the Labour movement.

Red Clydeside: born 1919.
Still alive?

Churchill campaigning in the Dundee seat he represented for many years

19 October 1922

Andrew Bonar Law became Prime Minister on the resignation of Lloyd George. The following month, his Conservative Party won a sizeable majority in the general election, which brought into parliament 29 MPs from Scotland who took the Labour whip, including 20 from the Independent Labour Party – the Red or Wild Clydesiders, as they were known. Bonar Law resigned and was replaced by Stanley Baldwin in May 1923 after contracting throat cancer. He died on 30 October that year.

30 November 1923

John Maclean, described as Scotland's greatest revolutionary, died of pneumonia. He was just 44. Although he never gained a parliamentary seat, his position at the heart of the Red Clydeside movement was undoubted, as he had taught many of its leaders their socialist theories. He was jailed several times for sedition, spending much of the First World War – which he condemned as anti-worker – in prison, where he was force-fed. Although his hard-line Scottish republican socialism had caused a break with many of his former allies, some 10,000 people attended his funeral, and his influence has remained greater than any of his actual achievements.

January 1924

After the Tories' defeat on a motion of confidence, Lossiemouth-born Ramsay MacDonald became Prime Minister, less than six years after losing his first seat in the Commons. He had returned as MP for Aberavon in 1922, and his sheer ability made him Labour's leader. His minority government had little chance of survival, however, and MacDonald famously said he was in office but not in power. The first Labour government was over within the year, the Tories winning easily in the October election after the infamous Zinoviev letter – giving British communists instructions on how to start a revolution – caused an anti-Labour backlash. In that election in Scotland, the Conservatives won 38 seats, Labour 26 and the Liberals nine, symbolic of their dramatic decline as Labour rose.

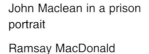

John Maclean in a prison portrait

Ramsay MacDonald

Churchill kept the Prince of Wales informed about the General Strike

3 May 1926

The General Strike began at midnight. The TUC had called the strike in support of the national miners' strike called against longer hours and pay cuts, and at first it received mass support, particularly in Scotland. Troops were deployed around the country and within days British society polarised on class lines, as the strike was demonised in such official 'newspapers' as the *British Gazette* (editor: Winston Churchill, then Chancellor of the Exchequer). With worker support dwindling, the TUC called off the strike on 12 May, but the miners fought on for six months before finally giving in and allowing the working day to be increased from seven to eight hours.

April 1928

After the failure of the Reverend James Barr's bill for Scottish self-government, the National Party of Scotland was founded, with its activists drawn mainly from the Scottish Home Rule Association, including Robert Bontine Cunninghame Graham.

On 30 May 1929 Labour won the general election, the first in which all men and women over 21 could vote. With insufficient seats for an outright majority, Ramsay MacDonald formed a minority government with Liberal support. Its members included Oswald Mosley, who resigned from the cabinet a year later.

The Depression and the rise of fascism marked the following decade. Oswald Mosley and his fascists never really caught on in Scotland, although some in the aristocracy and middle classes flirted with the cause. On his first visit to Scotland in September 1931, Mosley was chased from Glasgow Green and stoned by his opponents; he rarely returned.

An unhealthy sectarianism also marked Scottish politics and local government in particular during the '30s, with candidates standing and winning on anti-Catholic tickets in both Glasgow and Edinburgh.

With Britain facing economic ruin, in August 1931 Ramsay MacDonald resigned as Labour Prime Minister but was asked to form a National Government. Called a traitor by his own party, MacDonald went to the polls in October and the largest landslide in election history gave his National Government 554 seats – 473 of them Tory. MacDonald then formed an uneasy alliance with Tory leader Stanley Baldwin until his resignation in 1935, when Baldwin took over. MacDonald died on a trip to America in 1937.

Soup kitchens: a common sight in Depression-hit Scotland

Below: A Scottish business club which, like so many, gave Mosleyite speeches a sympathetic hearing, only to turn against him when the true colours of fascism were revealed

Robert Bontine
Cunninghame Graham, first
president of Scotland's
Labour and National Parties
and celebrated writer,
traveller and horseman

7 April 1934

The Scottish National Party was founded from the amalgamation of the National
and Scottish Parties. The first President was the writer and former Liberal MP
Robert Bontine Cunninghame Graham. It was a largely intellectual movement at
first, and the SNP's prominent early members included Hugh MacDiarmid, the
Duke of Montrose and Glasgow lawyer 'King' John MacCormick.

Tom Johnston, Secretary of
State

1939–45

The wartime government was not simply concerned
with the fighting of the war. As early as 1942,
William Beveridge's report laid the foundations for
the National Health Service and the expansion of
the Welfare State. The following year saw pledges to
rebuild Britain's housing, and in 1944 R.A. Butler's
Education Bill promised great reforms. Pay As You
Earn tax was also introduced that year.

Under Tom Johnston, arguably Scotland's finest
Secretary of State and an ardent home ruler, the
Scottish Office became ever more important in the
affairs of the country. Johnston was not only a great
political organiser but also a visionary, and he set up
the North of Scotland Hydro Electricity Board,
which he later chaired.

Clement Attlee (centre) led Labour to the khaki election victory . . .

. . . in which the young Denis Healey was a candidate

April 1945

The Scottish National Party won its first seat in parliament, Robert McIntyre winning a by-election in Motherwell. He would hold the seat for only a few weeks. Dr McIntyre returned to prominence in the '60s, when he became Provost of Stirling. On 26 July 1945 Labour, under Clement Attlee, won the 'khaki election' with a majority of 173. The government announced plans to nationalise the Bank of England, road haulage and railways, the ports, the iron and steel industry, the mines and the electricity industry, and to establish the National Health Service.

22 March 1947

The Scottish Convention movement, brainchild of John MacCormick after his parting from the SNP, called a National Assembly which attracted 600 people from all walks of Scottish life. The government responded with a White Paper which promised more powers for the Scottish Grand Committee. By 1950 more than two million people had signed the Convention, a petition calling for home rule.

Fervent patriot Wendy Wood lit the fire of nationalist dissent

The Stone returns over the border a second time, some 26 years after Ian Hamilton and his fellows repatriated it

25 December 1950

On Christmas Day 1950, the Stone of Destiny was found to have been removed from under the Coronation Throne in Westminster Abbey. In what became the greatest *cause célèbre* of modern Scottish politics, a group of students led by Ian Hamilton, now a QC, took the Stone to Scotland. After a massive police search and international publicity, the 'Stone' was handed back, though it may have been a copy. The audacious deed put nationalism on the front pages and there was considerable anger – mostly in England – when Hamilton and his colleagues got off, so to speak, Scot free. The Stone was returned 26 years later in a mysterious move by Conservative Secretary of State Michael Forsyth.

Harold Macmillan at play

26 May 1955

A year after the Balfour Commission recommended no real changes to the governance of Scotland, the Conservatives swept to power in a general election in which they won 50.1 per cent of the vote in Scotland – the only time in the century such a 'popular majority' occurred. The sole Liberal MP was Orkney's Jo Grimond, who became leader of the UK party the following year. On 8 October 1959, despite the Suez disaster, the Conservatives under Harold Macmillan won the general election with an increased majority of 100, but in a recession-hit Scotland they lost five seats, the start of a long decline.

18 October 1963

The 14th Earl of Home, better known as Alec Douglas-Home, became Prime Minister on Harold Macmillan's resignation. He renounced his title and entered the Commons via a by-election in Perth, but then led his party to defeat in October the following year when Harold Wilson was adjudged the better television performer.

Douglas-Home resigned as party leader in 1965 but returned as Foreign Secretary in the Heath government before becoming, once again, Lord Home, this time as a life peer following his retirement in 1974.

31 March 1966

After toiling with a minimal majority, Harold Wilson called a snap election and was rewarded with an overall majority of 96. William Ross became Secretary of State for Scotland again.

On 2 November 1967, in the month that Harold Wilson devalued the pound, the most famous by-election in Scottish history saw Glasgow solicitor Winnie Ewing win Hamilton for the SNP, overturning a majority of 16,500 for victory by 1,800 votes. Both major parties responded with alarm. The following year Edward Heath proposed the creation of a Scottish Assembly, while Wilson set up the Kilbrandon Commission to look at the governance of Scotland. It finally reported in 1973, by which time Heath was PM, Britain was set to join the EEC and the country was beset with major industrial strife, led by the miners.

Harold Wilson and some fab friends

Winnie Ewing wins at Hamilton

T.HUTTON   M.RIFKIND   I.CHISHOLM   B.TATTERSALL

UNIVERSITY OF EDINBURGH

All our yesterdays: Chancellor of the Exchequer Gordon Brown as student rector at Edinburgh; Sir Malcolm Rifkind representing Edinburgh on *University Challenge* . . .

February and October 1974

After the three-day week provoked by the miners' strike, Ted Heath called a snap election, hoping for a mandate for his policies. Labour narrowly failed to win an overall majority but Harold Wilson returned as Prime Minister. He called a second election in October, when, fighting on the ticket 'It's Scotland's Oil' after the discovery of oil in the North Sea, the SNP boosted their vote to win a record 11 seats and 30 per cent of the Scottish vote. Wilson's narrow overall majority meant that the government rapidly conceded the principle of devolution for Scotland and Wales, and a bill was soon brought before the Commons.

11 February 1975

Margaret Thatcher replaced Edward Heath as Conservative leader. Addressing the party in Glasgow, she said that an assembly 'must be a top priority to ensure more decisions are taken in Scotland for Scotsmen'. But by December 1976, after James Callaghan had taken over as Prime Minister on the sudden resignation of Harold Wilson, the Tories decided to try and kill the Scotland and Wales bill in a bid to bring down the government. Malcolm Rifkind and Alick Buchanan-Smith resigned from the shadow cabinet in disgust, and another 40 Conservative MPs abstained.

On 25 January 1978, the arrival of the Lib-Lab pact brought about a new Scotland bill, with a referendum on devolution as the main target. On Burns Night, Scots-born Labour MP for Islington George Cunningham succeeded with an amendment that effectively meant 40 per cent of the Scottish population had to vote 'yes' for devolution to proceed. Tam Dalyell, Labour's maverick MP, also framed the West Lothian Question, asking, in short, why Scottish MPs should be allowed to vote on English issues and not vice versa.

On 1 March 1979, after campaigns which involved strange bedfellows on both sides, the referendum produced a majority in favour of devolution, but as it was only 32.9 per cent of the electorate, the target had been missed. Devolution was effectively

. . . Tam Dalyell as a young MP . . .

. . . William Whitelaw putting the Conservative case . . .

. . . and John Smith arguing for a Yes vote in 1979

dead in the water. The SNP later refused all-party talks to try and save Callaghan's government; he famously called them 'turkeys voting for Christmas'. In May 1979, Margaret Thatcher and the Conservatives swept to power and the SNP were reduced to just two seats.

The years of Conservative rule under Margaret Thatcher are often characterised with simplicity as a bad time for Scotland. The government's near-absolute refusal to bale out weak businesses meant that Scotland was first into recession and took longer to come out of it than any other part of Britain. It also meant, however, that the economy was forced to diversify into such areas as electronics and financial services, which have proved relatively stable. The Thatcherite government also made many mistakes, the introduction of the poll tax chief among them. By September 1989, its unpopularity meant that some 300,000 people in Strathclyde alone had defaulted on their payment of the tax, yet it is often forgotten that the tax was introduced as an experiment in Scotland because the rates system had become so discredited in the public view.

Lack of opportunities for opposition also made local authorities into political battlegrounds, with councils like Labour-controlled Edinburgh and Stirling defying the government, though in the long run Labour's hold over local government proved unhealthy for the party. At first, however, the opposition was divided – the formation of the SDP and its later Alliance with the Liberals split Labour, though less so in Scotland than elsewhere. The SNP also went through a period of internal strife over its political philosophy.

But over the years, undoubtedly the biggest cause of anger with the Thatcher government was the 'democratic deficit' which saw the Conservatives reduced to just 11 seats from its previous 21 in Scotland in the 1987 general election. Margaret Thatcher seemed unable to understand Scotland and vice versa; perhaps the defining moment was her 'Sermon on the Mound' speech to the General Assembly of the Church of Scotland in May 1988, which outraged the clerics with its praise of wealth-gaining.

That year saw several crucial events. The publi-

The spin doctors did not notice this sign

Nor could they do anything about these protests

The heat of picket-line
protests

An issue which united so
many

Society's divisions writ large

Before 'that' General
Assembly speech

cation of the Claim of Right began the work of the Scottish Constitutional
Convention, which eventually produced a blueprint for a devolved Scotland.
Within Labour, an important pro-devolution grouping called Scottish Labour
Action was set up, and the party's often-lukewarm approach to home rule issues
hardened into committed support for devolution as a means of combating sepa-
ratism. Meanwhile, internal strife within the Conservatives at UK level was
mounting and, facing defeat in a leadership election, on 22 November 1990
Margaret Thatcher resigned as Prime Minister and leader of the Conservatives to
be replaced by John Major. Her international reputation remained intact, and
despite her uneasy relationship with Scotland, there can be no doubting her
extraordinary effect on Britain as a whole. She changed politics for ever.

The Fifers united will never be defeated

A man who could take a joke, even from Stephen Fry

He lies on Iona in the company of kings

9 April 1992

With the clamour for reform growing, *The Scotsman* published a poll in January which suggested that 50 per cent of the Scottish people favoured independence. It was perhaps the newspaper's single biggest contribution to Scottish politics in the twentieth century, and it is difficult to overstate the electrifying effect which the poll had in Scotland and further afield. *The Scotsman* followed the poll with a memorable televised public debate involving the four Scottish party leaders, which ensured that constitutional reform would take centre stage in the forthcoming election, in which John Major duly played the 'Union card', arguing against the break-up of the UK. The result in Scotland, as in the UK as a whole, mystified the opposition – the Tory share of the vote in Scotland actually increased, if only by 1.6 per cent overall.

Although the Tories stopped short of privatising Scotland's water supply, massive reform of local government, scrapping the Labour bastions of the regional councils which had been established only in 1975, did go ahead. Scotland also suffered less in the '90s' recession than England; for the first time in a generation, Scottish unemployment was below the UK average.

12 May 1994

John Smith, a Scottish lawyer, had replaced Neil Kinnock as Labour leader and had begun the often-difficult process of reforming the Labour Party in the UK. He called devolution the 'settled will' of the Scottish people and referred to constitutional reform as 'unfinished business'. He was regarded as the king in waiting, but died of a massive heart attack in his London flat. His death provoked genuine upset on all sides of the political establishment and a show of public grief unprecedented for a politician.

1995–97

Smith's death, which had brought Tony Blair into the Labour leadership, provoked a crisis for the party in Scotland, where the Monklands East by-election was tarred with allegations of sectarianism in the area's local authorities. It was the beginning of a painful process of scrutiny of Labour local government which is still continuing.

In January 1995, *Scotland on Sunday* broke the story that SNP leader Alex Salmond favoured devolution as a stepping stone to independence – a major change in policy that paved the way for future co-operation with the other pro-devolution parties. Later that year, a Hollywood movie about the life of William Wallace based on a historically inaccurate script created a new political phenomenon known as the Braveheart effect, which has been defined as Scots being made aware of their culture. It even appeared to affect Tory Secretary of State Michael Forsyth, the Thatcherite arch-unionist who had proved typically adept in wrong-footing his opponents with a number of new, almost devolutionary initiatives. It was he who arranged for the Stone of Destiny to be returned to Scotland from Westminster in the dying months of the Major government. It was to no avail, however. On 1 May 1997, Labour swept to power with their biggest landslide victory since 1945. The Conservatives lost every seat in Scotland. Tony Blair, born in Scotland and a product of Fettes College, Edinburgh, became Prime Minister, flanked by Gordon Brown as Chancellor and Robin Cook as Foreign Secretary.

Things, they said, could only get better

Symbols of Scotland. And a Chancellor

11 September 1997

Despite huge controversy and the anger of the Scottish Constitutional Convention, Labour had committed itself to a referendum on devolution asking two questions of the Scottish people: did they want a Scottish Parliament and should it have tax-varying powers? After a White Paper was published outlining the devolutionary scheme, an unprecedented alliance of Labour, SNP and Liberal Democrats campaigned for a double 'yes' vote. The majority on the first question was never in doubt, and shortly after 4.30 a.m. on 12 September the national count in Edinburgh saw the majority also reached on the second question. Devolution was now inevitable,

Opposite: The day of decision dawned happily

and the final shape of the parliament was determined in the long passage through the Commons and Lords of the Scotland Act 1998.

1 July 1999

The first Scottish parliamentary election on 6 May produced no outright winner, while proportional representation as proposed by the Scottish Constitutional Convention gave minority parties such as the Scottish Socialists and the Greens a seat in parliament. After days of negotiations, Labour and the Liberal Democrats agreed to form the Scottish Executive. The Conservatives had made gains from their nadir of 1997, but the second-placed SNP formed the official opposition. The parliament convened in the General Assembly building – the new building in Holyrood will not be ready until 2001 – and the early days proved fraught, with much criticism of the new MSPs' performance and rows which show signs at least of healthy debate.

On 1 July the Queen performed the opening ceremony, on a day which featured rock concerts, fly-pasts, a children's procession, a memorable rendition of Robert Burns's 'A Man's a Man for A' That' and a stirring speech by First Minister Donald Dewar, the former Secretary of State and the chief architect of devolution. His words are a suitable ending to this chronicle:

'"There shall be a Scottish parliament". Through long years, those words were

Some battled with buses

Others used old friends and a lucky dip

Some grinned their way through it

But eventually the Parliament was formed

Despite all the fears beforehand, it was a day that some will never forget

It was a day when some spoke as if inspired; when one's love of Scotland shone through . . .

first a hope, then a belief, then a promise. Now they are a reality. This is a moment anchored in our history. Today we reach back through the long haul to win this parliament, through the struggles of those who brought democracy to Scotland, to that other parliament dissolved in controversy nearly three centuries ago.

'Today we look forward to the time when this moment will be seen as a turning point: the day when democracy was renewed in Scotland, when we revitalised our place in this, our United Kingdom.'

. . . and when centuries of longing were fulfilled

WAR AND CONFLICT

Throughout the twentieth century, Scottish soldiers, sailors, pilots and auxiliary forces have been at the forefront of the defence of Britain. Latterly they have also played their part in NATO and United Nations peacekeeping initiatives.

BOER WAR

17 May 1900

The relief of Mafeking, held by troops under Colonel Baden-Powell, after a 217-day siege was later seen as the turning point in the Boer War, in which the British Army had suffered numerous reversals. Field Marshal Lord Roberts had taken command of the British forces in January, and had brought with him Sir Hector Archibald MacDonald, son of a Dingwall crofter, who had uniquely risen through the ranks to become a major-general.

Known as 'Fighting Mac', General MacDonald led the Highland Brigade in some of the most daring and successful exploits of the war, including long marches across the veldt in pursuit of Boer leaders. Two years later he died by his own hand in a Paris hotel after mysterious accusations were made against him while he commanded the British forces in Ceylon. On 31 May 1902, the Treaty of Vereeniging ended the Boer War. Only later was it revealed that the war had cost 100,000 military and civilian casualties.

Below: 'Fighting Mac'

Right: Some of the troops he led march off to the Boer War

THE FIRST WORLD WAR

28 June 1914

After years of sabre-rattling across Europe, Serbian student Gavrilo Princip assassinated Archduke Franz Ferdinand, heir to the Austro-Hungarian throne, and his wife in Sarajevo. Events moved with astonishing rapidity afterwards. On 28 July Austria declared war on Serbia, whose ally Russia promptly mobilised her troops. On 2 August the German Kaiser declared war on Russia after his cousin the Czar refused his demand to cease mobilisation. France being aligned with Russia, the Kaiser then declared war on the French and the Royal Navy was mobilised.

4 August 1914

At the end of a Bank Holiday weekend in which Belgium had been invaded by Germany, Britain declared war on the Kaiser and his people in line with the Treaty of London, 1839, in which Britain had guaranteed Belgian neutrality. Inside a fortnight the British Expeditionary Force, including a large contingent of Scottish troops, left for France, but within six days the Battle of Mons ended in defeat for the British.

September 1914

Recruiting fever was at its height as the conviction grew that the war would be 'over by Christmas', especially after the successes of the Battle of the Marne. In one month alone, 20,000 men enlisted in Glasgow, most of them for the Highland Light Infantry, the city's own regiment, which eventually raised 26 battalions.

Home by Christmas: Glasgow 'Highlanders' march off to war

Germans pictured during that extraordinary Christmas truce . . .

. . . in which the singing of hymns was led by Major Buchanan-Dunlop

25 December 1914

In one of the most bizarre occurrences of the war, the opposing troops declared a Christmas truce in no-man's-land. Major Buchanan-Dunlop, formerly of Loretto School in Musselburgh, led the singing of hymns.

1915

By August, more than a million men were on active service on the Western Front, where casualties already exceeded 300,000. In December, a Scot, Sir Douglas Haig, took over as commander-in-chief of British forces on the Western Front. He has been blamed for poor British leadership and the war of attrition in the trenches, though in truth those tactics had already been established.

Protecting against gas, first used by the Germans at Ypres

6 January 1916

Conscription was introduced despite much opposition. In Glasgow, munitions workers went on strike in protest and in March six of the strike leaders on the Clyde Workers' Committee were arrested and imprisoned. Throughout the war, workers' leaders on the Clyde and elsewhere were jailed for sedition. As the country moved to full war production, it was revealed that two million women had been employed in the past year alone.

April 1916

After years of relatively minor actions, the Easter Rising in Dublin signalled the beginning of a much greater armed conflict for Irish independence.

5 June 1916

Just a few days after the Battle of Jutland confined the German fleet to harbour, Lord Kitchener, virtual creator of the British Army in the Great War and the face on the country's recruiting posters, was killed when the cruiser HMS *Hampshire* struck a mine off Orkney and sank with all hands. Then, on 1 July, the Battle of the Somme began with the worst day in British military history. Some 60,000 casualties were suffered, and by the end of August the total fatalities were 127,000, or 20 per cent of all war deaths. Haig then rushed a new invention, the tank, into action, despite justified fears that it was not ready.

6 April 1917

Germany's submarine campaign against neutral ships was one of the main reasons for the declaration of war by the USA. In August 1917, a British offensive became bogged down in the mud of Flanders, while aeroplanes were used to bomb ground troops. Later that autumn, the Russians and Italians both suffered heavy defeats, but on the Western Front the Allies were gradually getting the upper hand.

Munitions factories in Glasgow were often prone to industrial action as the war was not popular everywhere . . .

. . . especially after conscription forced most able-bodied men into the ranks

A submarine of the K class similar to those which sank in the Gareloch and the Firth of Forth

31 January 1918

In a disastrous naval exercise in the Firth of Forth, two submarines were lost and several ships damaged in a nightmarish series of accidents that cost the lives of 103 sailors. These 'friendly fire' losses added to the previous year's mysterious loss of the submarine *K13* in the Gareloch, an incident in which 32 men died.

April 1918 onwards

A huge German offensive threatened the Allies all along the Western Front. Another attack in July became Germany's last push to win the war, but it was repulsed. The final great offensive by the Allies began with the 'black day for Germany' on 8 August. Within weeks German resistance collapsed and their demoralised troops began surrendering in great numbers, while others fell back to the original Hindenburg line of defence.

A German battleship lies
scuttled in Scapa Flow

11 November 1918

At the 11th hour of the 11th day of the 11th month, the Armistice took effect.
Britain and its empire had lost more than a million people. More than 100,000
Scotsmen died in action, with more than 50,000 of these in the Highland
Division. Scotland's losses were acknowledged to be disproportionately higher
than those of any other country in the empire.

21 June 1919

The German fleet was scuttled in Scapa Flow on the orders of Admiral von
Reuter. More than 70 ships went down.

THE SECOND WORLD WAR

3 September 1939

The long years of appeasement of Hitler's Nazis had failed, though they had bought time for Britain to re-arm. After the invasion of Poland, Prime Minister Neville Chamberlain read his speech declaring war from the cabinet room on the morning of Sunday, 3 September. The declaration took place while many Scots were at church. Two days previously, the largest mass evacuation of children ever seen in Scotland had been carried out with great efficiency. Glasgow, Edinburgh, Dundee, Clydebank and Rosyth were effectively emptied of their youngsters, who were billeted on families in rural towns and villages around the country. The ill health and filthy condition of many of the children from Glasgow in particular caused a scandal.

Preparations for the civilian population to meet the threat of war had been going on for months, with the issuing of gas masks and the preparation of air-raid shelters and the blackout a priority. RAF reconnaissance showed that at first the blackout was 'very unsatisfactory', as *The Scotsman* reported.

The arrival of enemy action was immediate. Within hours of Chamberlain's announcement, a U-boat sank the Glasgow-registered, Clyde-built liner *Athenia* 200 miles west of the Hebrides with the loss of 112 lives.

Mass evacuation of children took place over the first weekend of September 1939

Gas-mask drill replaced ordinary lessons at school

Opposite: For some it was an adventure

The men of 602 and 603 sqaudrons

They received royal recognition for their feats . . .

. . . which included the downing of this Heinkel bomber, the first to crash-land on British soil

October 1939

The full horror of the war was brought home dramatically to Scotland in the space of 48 hours. First, the sinking of the *Royal Oak* at the so-called impregnable anchorage of Scapa Flow in the Orkneys on 14 October cost more than 800 lives. Two days later came the first German air raid on British soil. A contingent of German bombers attacked shipping in the Forth and the Rosyth anchorage. Four German planes were shot down and seven sailors killed. Although the honour of claiming the first 'kill' of the war went to 603 City of Edinburgh squadron, it was their colleagues in 602 City of Glasgow squadron who went into shooting action first.

On 28 October, both squadrons combined to shoot down a Heinkel 111 over East Lothian, the first German plane to crash-land on British soil. These Auxiliary Air Force squadrons were called into full service and later fought with great distinction in the Battle of Britain. On 13 November, the first bombs to fall on British soil landed on Shetland.

January 1940

Rationing of some foodstuffs was introduced. Rationing of one sort or another continued until 1954.

May/June 1940

Men of the 51st Highland Division were among many thousands
of British troops cut off by the swift advance of the German forces
through Belgium and northern France. Two out of three brigades
were surrounded at St Valery and captured, though many Scottish
troops were among those who escaped at Dunkirk, where one of
the brave flotilla of little ships was the original paddle steamer
Waverley, sunk during the evacuation.

By July 1940, thousands of Scots, particularly former servicemen, had rushed to join the Local Defence Volunteers after they
were formed in May. In July they were renamed the Home Guard.

September 1940

Having lost the Battle of Britain, the Luftwaffe began the blitz on
British cities and major towns. Glasgow had first been bombed a
year earlier. By the end of the war, all of Scotland's cities plus
Clydebank, Greenock, Dumbarton, Fraserburgh, Peterhead and
Montrose would suffer bombing raids, with many other areas hit
by either stray or dumped bombs or one-off German raiders.

Over two nights in March 1941, Clydebank was targeted by
the Luftwaffe, supposedly in a bid to destroy the shipyards and factories, though
in reality the civilian population bore the brunt of the raid. In the town and surrounding areas, an estimated 1,200 people were killed. Only eight houses out of
12,000 in Clydebank were undamaged and 37,000 people were made homeless.
From 5 May to 7 May, the Luftwaffe turned its attention to the lower Clyde.
Dumbarton, Port Glasgow and Gourock were all hit, but Greenock took the
worst pounding. Hundreds died and more than half the houses in the town were

At first they were just Local
Defence Volunteers . . .

. . . and then they became
the Home Guard

Below: The wreckage of
Rudolf Hess's
Messerschmitt 110

damaged, with 1,000 homes destroyed.

Shortly afterwards, on 10 May 1941, in one of the most bizarre incidents of the war, Hitler's deputy Rudolf Hess, by this time perhaps mentally unbalanced, landed near Eaglesham after flying his Messerschmitt 110 from Germany. On his own initiative, he was carrying a peace offer to the Duke of Hamilton, a fellow airman whom he had met before the war. Jailed as a war criminal, he committed suicide in Spandau prison in 1987.

7 December 1941

Following Pearl Harbor, Japanese forces swiftly marched through Asia, imprisoning thousands of British troops including many Scottish soldiers and expatriates in Hong Kong, Singapore and elsewhere.

On 15 November 1942, for the first time in the war, church bells were rung to celebrate victory after General Montgomery led the Allied troops, including a rebuilt Highland Division, to success at El Alamein. The Allies' invasion of North Africa and the simultaneous counterstrikes by Russia on the Eastern Front showed that the tide of the war was turning.

In July 1943, the successful invasion of Sicily led to Italian surrender within two months. The fiercest resistance by the German forces in Italy was at Monte Cassino, where the Scots Guards played a prominent role. On 6 June 1944, with the Axis forces in retreat everywhere, the D-Day landings in Normandy breached Hitler's Fortress Europe once and for all. One of the bravest actions on D-Day was that of Lord Lovat and his commandos, who fought their way inland to meet up with paratroops at the vital Pegasus Bridge. In the weeks that followed, the Highland Division played a vital role in the consolidation of the invasion and breakout from Normandy.

Churchill inspects preparations for D-Day

Lord Lovat and his commandos pictured on D-Day

With pipes blaring, Scottish troops fought their way to the heart of Germany

8 May 1945

After the collapse of German resistance and the suicide of Hitler, unconditional surrender was signed by the German High Command at 2.41 a.m. on 7 May. The following day was declared Victory in Europe day and hundreds of thousands of Scots took to the streets to celebrate, with George Square and Princes Street both engulfed.

They also fought who
stayed behind and raised
cash for the war effort

Women in uniform – a
common sight in Scotland
in the 1940s

2 September 1945

After the atomic bombing of Hiroshima and Nagasaki, the official celebration of victory over Japan, VJ day, ended the Second World War.

Although mass demobilisation was almost immediate, the ramifications of the war meant that Scottish troops were forced to serve as members of the occupying forces in Germany and elsewhere and occasionally met violent ends, particularly at the hands of the Zionist guerrillas in Palestine.

1950–53

The invasion of South Korea by the Communist north began a conflict which at one time threatened to turn the Cold War very hot. Scottish troops fought in the Commonwealth forces under United Nations commander General Douglas MacArthur, who was replaced midway through the conflict by General Mark Clark. After two million deaths, mostly among the civilian population, the war ended in July 1953.

1950s and 1960s

The break-up of the British Empire was largely peaceful, but in Cyprus, Kenya, Malaya and elsewhere there were prolonged conflicts with native insurgents. Scottish troops saw service in all of these emergencies. In October and November 1956, the Suez crisis saw troops from Britain and France invade the Canal Zone, led by paratroops and the Royal Marines, only for them to leave in humiliating

Scottish troops go ashore to fight in the Korean War

Kosovo, 1999, and the sight which greeted Scottish peacekeeping troops and *The Scotsman*'s photographer

circumstances shortly afterwards when the US refused to support the action.

1967

In Aden, which ceased to be a British colony in November that year, Colonel Colin 'Mad Mitch' Mitchell of the Argyll and Sutherland Highlanders briefly became Britain's most famous soldier with his tough and cool handling of the conflict with local Arab insurgents. His actions included marching the Argylls into Aden with bayonets fixed and bagpipes blaring.

1969 to present day

The present Northern Ireland troubles began in August 1969 when civil-rights marchers provoked sectarian conflict and troops were sent in to restore order. Since then, many thousands of Scottish troops have served in Northern Ireland, where the regiments take their turn on a rota basis.

March/June 1982

The invasion of the Falkland Islands by Argentina led to a risky but ultimately successful conflict in which the Scots Guards played a vital role with their capture of the strategically vital Mount Tumbledown, a battle in which they sustained 50 casualties. This was the last pitched battle fought by Scottish troops on soil under British sovereignty.

16 January 1991

Iraq invaded its oil-rich neighbour Kuwait in August 1990 and a unique coalition of Western and Arab forces massed in Saudi Arabia to try and force Iraqi President Saddam Hussein to withdraw. Despite intense diplomatic and military pressure, he refused, and Operation Desert Storm, the Gulf War, began, with five weeks of incessant air raids and missile bombardment. Late on 23 February, Allied tanks, artillery and troops poured into Kuwait under immense and unchallenged air cover. Exactly 100 hours later the war was over and Iraq's forces were in full flight for home, with much of their armour destroyed and tens of thousands of troops in Allied custody. Scottish soldiers, pilots and sailors played their part, with the Territorials being called up at home to assist in the operation. Sadly, the single greatest British loss of life came in a 'friendly fire' incident when two American A-10 aircraft attacked British armoured vehicles, killing nine soldiers including men of the Queen's Own Highlanders. It is estimated that the Iraqi dead numbered 50,000.

The various Balkans conflicts have seen Scottish forces used several times in United Nations or NATO peacekeeping roles, the latest being in Kosovo in 1999.

THE ARTS OF EVERY KIND

A rare edition of the first Edinburgh Festival programme in 1947

The arts in Scotland are now hugely diverse and previous misconceptions about Scottish attitudes to the arts have been set aside by their progress over the past 100 years. The following passages chart a brief history of the major developments in the twentieth century.

Two events can be singled out as major turning points in a century of cultural reawakening. First, the foundation of the Edinburgh Festival in 1947 was a small country's declaration of faith in civilisation after the dark days of the Second World War, and that gamble paid off. Second, in the 1980s, many people outside Glasgow openly derided its nomination as the European City of Culture 1990, but the criticism turned to cheers as Glasgow carried off its year as cultural capital with unparalleled style and success, cultural rebirth being perhaps the main theme of the century.

By any objective standards, Scotland's arts scene and cultural life in general is in far better shape than that which greeted the start of the twentieth century, and the advent of the National Lottery in the 1990s has guaranteed that there will at least be funding for 'new directions' in the arts, the name chosen by the Scottish Arts Council for its scheme to support artists. The Council is the quango through which state aid for the arts is channelled, and was founded as recently as 1967 after 20 years as the Scottish Committee of the Arts Council of Great Britain.

Perhaps the clearest sign of the good health of Scotland's cultural scene was the opening on St Andrew's Day 1998 of the new £65 million Museum of Scotland. Its design by architects Benson and Forsyth was controversial, and Prince Charles famously resigned as Patron of the National Museums because of his dislike of the planned building. The new building, however, has become a symbol of an overall Scottish cultural renaissance and crowds have flocked to see the exhibits which have helped to make up the history of Scotland.

Kathleen Ferrier's recital during that first Festival

LITERATURE

From the 1920s onwards, the Scottish Renaissance was the dominant movement in Scottish literature and perhaps the most influential upheaval in all the cultural activity of Scotland in the twentieth century.

The phrase 'Scottish Renaissance' was coined in 1924 by a French professor, Denis Saurat, who wrote how poets and writers in Scotland had overthrown the Victorian kailyard school of writing which still largely dominated Scottish literature in the early part of the 1900s. The principal creator of the Renaissance was the poet Hugh MacDiarmid, Christopher Murray Grieve, the publication of whose long poem 'A Drunk Man Looks at a Thistle' in 1926 was arguably the high point of the movement.

MacDiarmid aimed to revive the ancient Scots language in the form of Lallans, Lowland Scots, which some people – such as the poet Edwin Muir – saw as artificial. After decades of remarkable poetry, incessant argument and political radicalism that saw him expelled from both the Communist and the Scottish National Parties, Hugh MacDiarmid became recognised internationally as Scotland's greatest literary figure of the century. He died in 1978, and afterwards his friend, the poet Norman MacCaig, suggested he should be remembered not by silence but by 'two minutes' pandemonium'.

MacCaig himself was arguably Scotland's greatest poet writing in English, and he won the Queen's Gold Medal for poetry in 1986, near the end of his long career which featured most memorably the poetic cycle 'A Man in Assynt'. With MacDiarmid and the Gaelic poet Sorley MacLean (Somhairle MacGill-Eain), MacCaig formed a triumvirate of grand old men of letters, the last two surviving their colleague into the 1990s. MacLean was several times touted as a potential winner of the Nobel Prize for literature, so influential was his poetry.

The Scottish Renaissance attracted many followers around Scotland. One was the Perth poet William Soutar, who produced remarkable work from his sick bed. His 'Diary of a Dying Man', recording his last days in 1943, is an inspirational work. Sydney Goodsir Smith (1915–75) and Robert Garioch Sutherland (1909–81) were two Edinburgh-based poets heavily influenced by MacDiarmid who both produced classic works in Scots.

Other poets and writers such as Muir and his protégé, the Orcadian George Mackay Brown, enjoyed long, varied and fruitful careers and influenced great poets in other countries, such as Seamus Heaney and Ted Hughes. In more recent times, Edwin Morgan and Tom Leonard among others have celebrated the poetic rhythms of Glasgow life, while the former is a noted translator who achieved a memorable triumph with his rendering into Scots of *Cyrano de Bergerac*.

In 1999, poetry's revival in Scotland was set in stone with the opening of the new Scottish Poetry Library in Edinburgh, the brainchild and lifelong cause of the poet Tessa Ransford.

The head of Hugh MacDiarmid, famously moulded by Benno Schotz during a ground-breaking BBC Scotland programme

MacDiarmid with his great friend Norman MacCaig

Glasgow's miles brighter –
Edwin Morgan, the city's
first poet laureate, in
sunglasses

Dame Naomi Mitchison and
George Mackay Brown
enjoy a quiet moment in
Edinburgh

The Scottish Renaissance saw novelists, too, begin to employ a distinctive Scottish voice. Even before MacDiarmid began his work, two notable exceptions to the kailyard canon were *The House with the Green Shutters* and *Gillespie*, novels by George Douglas Brown and John MacDougall Hay, published in 1901 and 1914 respectively. Both featured overpowering male central characters and, curiously, both authors died – in 1902 and 1919 respectively – shortly after their books became successful.

The same fate awaited James Leslie Mitchell (Lewis Grassic Gibbon), who died tragically young in 1935 shortly after completing his masterpiece *A Scots Quair*, a trilogy which includes *Sunset Song*, arguably the single most popular Scottish book of the century. Although he wrote in English, the MacDiarmid-influenced Mitchell accurately conveyed the language of his native north-east Scotland, while Neil M. Gunn, a personal friend of MacDiarmid, superbly evoked his Highland background in novels such as *Morning Tide*, *Highland River* and *The Silver Darlings*.

While writers such as George Blake and Neil Munro (Hugh Foulis) wrote of Glasgow and the west coast, the latter in his *Para Handy* novels, it was an Edinburgh woman who became the most important Scottish novelist of the century. *The Prime of Miss Jean Brodie* was Dame Muriel Spark's sixth novel and catapulted her to international fame, though such novels as *Memento Mori*, *The Ballad of Peckham Rye* and *The Bachelors* had already made her name. Although now living in Italy, and a convert to Roman Catholicism, she remains proud of her Scottish roots.

Dame Muriel Spark's lead ensured that the more recent generation of Scottish or Scottish-based novelists includes several women who have written on universal themes with a Scottish background, including Jessie Kesson, Joan Lingard, Candia McWilliam, Janice Galloway, A.L. Kennedy and Kate Atkinson. Nor is this a new phenomenon – Dame Naomi Mitchison's greatest success came in 1947 when she set aside her mythological themes to write *The Bull Calves*, a novel set firmly in her own family's history in Perthshire.

The trend of writing on Scottish and also foreign themes was probably started by Sir Compton Mackenzie, who wrote about life in the English theatre in *Carnival* before mixing humorous novels based in the Hebrides with serious books – so realistic that the government censored them – based on his time in military intelligence. Eric Linklater and James Kennaway, killed at the age of just 40 in a road accident in 1968, based works both in Scotland and elsewhere. The prolific Allan Massie's best-known novel featured the Roman emperor Augustus, while Robin Jenkins is equally at home in mythical Afghanistan and modern Scotland. Iain Banks mixes fantasy with well-worked Scottish themes such as the rites of passage undergone by Prentice McHoan in *The Crow Road*, and he also produces science fiction under the name Iain M. Banks. Glasgow's Ronald Frame set one of his best novels, *Sandmouth People*, entirely in an English coastal town.

The ability to move between different forms of writing is another common Scottish trait. Iain Crichton Smith has written prose and poetry in English and Gaelic, with most of his works having Highland settings, while William McIlvanney has mixed tough detective fiction with novels depicting the often harsh reality of life in west central Scotland. Addressing that latter theme in a different style, James Kelman produced Booker Prize-winning fiction, while Irvine Welsh's phenomenal success resulted from books set in uncharted territory for many novelists – the lowlife

Sir Arthur Conan Doyle

drugs scene in Edinburgh. Artist and novelist Alasdair Gray has written and illustrated some of the most original fiction of the century, with his masterpiece *Lanark* finally being published to great acclaim in 1981 after decades of preparation.

Critics, biographers and lexicographers have also flourished. The work of literature which took the longest to come to fruition in the twentieth century was *The Scottish National Dictionary*, first proposed by Sir William Alexander Craigie in 1919, begun in 1929 and completed in 1976.

Catherine Carswell's biography of Burns prompted a vehemently negative reaction when published in 1930 but was later recognised as a seminal work in the ongoing evaluation of the poet's life and influence. Alan Bold's 1988 biography of MacDiarmid eclipsed its author's own poetry.

Throughout the past 100 years, Scotland has also produced a succession of storytelling novelists whose work may not have been classed as high literature but who sold books by the million. Sir Arthur Conan Doyle, John Buchan, A.J. Cronin and Alistair MacLean were all at one time or another the best-selling writers in the world.

Popular novelists such as Ian Rankin, author of the Rebus detective novels, continue to enjoy success based on works set in Scotland, while George MacDonald Fraser borrowed the quintessential English anti-hero Flashman for a series of best-selling novels. For output, however, none can match Nigel Tranter, 90-year-old author of more than 100 books, mainly on Scottish historical themes, although given her extraordinary success in the final months of the century, it may well be that Harry Potter author Joanne K. Rowling will outsell them all.

PAINTING AND SCULPTURE

The biggest controversy of the twentieth century affecting Scottish art was not about the artworks themselves, but about the location of a gallery to display those Scottish works which cannot be seen because there are simply too many of them to be shown in public. The aim of the proposed National Gallery of Scottish Art is to showcase the massive national collection of Scottish painting and sculpture. Throughout the 1990s it appeared set to become a reality after Glasgow 'outbid' Edinburgh as potential host to the gallery. Sadly, the project is in abeyance following the failure of a multi-million-pound National Lottery bid.

The major cause of progress in painting and sculpture was the establishment over a 20-year period before the First World War of Scotland's four main art colleges. After years of development, Glasgow School of Art moved into a purpose-built building designed by Charles Rennie Mackintosh in 1895. Mackintosh later became one of the most important figures of Scottish art and architecture, and his reputation has both survived and been revived through succeeding generations. Edinburgh College of Art opened in 1909, followed by Gray's in Aberdeen and Duncan of Jordanstone's College in Dundee.

After the turn of the century the 'Glasgow Boys' such as James Guthrie, John Lavery and W.Y. MacGregor were the dominant school in Scottish art in association with the Glasgow style promoted by Mackintosh. Originally anti-establishment, two of the Glasgow Boys, Guthrie and Lavery, were later knighted. After the First World War, the group of painters known as the Scottish Colourists – S.J. Peploe, J.D. Fergusson, F.C.B. Cadell and G.L. Hunter – were the greatest influence on Scottish art. After them came a loosely associated group of equally influential artists with connections to Edinburgh College of Art, which included

Charles Rennie Mackintosh

Amanda Boyes of auctioneers Sotheby's holds a painting by 'Glasgow Boy' F.C.B. Cadell during a recent sale of Scottish art

William McTaggart, Anne Redpath, William Gillies and John Maxwell, all painting in different styles but sharing the same artistic ideals. Though Dublin-born, Phoebe Anna Traquair left her mark on Scottish art before her death in 1936 with her magnificent murals in various Edinburgh churches, and her reputation in the arts and crafts movement was such that in 1920 she became the first woman member of the Royal Scottish Academy.

An exquisite piece of Phoebe Anna Traquair's jewellery

Before and after the Second World War, artists such as Joan Eardley, who died tragically young in 1963 at the age of 42, and John Houston developed their own style of landscape painting, while William Johnstone developed the idea of a Scottish painting renaissance to match that in literature pioneered by his friend Hugh MacDiarmid. Abstract painters such as William Gear and Alan Davie were far more famous abroad than in their native land, a fate which has also befallen John Bellany and painters/sculptors Ian Hamilton Finlay and Sir Eduardo Paolozzi. The latter's own collection of his sculptures forms the backbone of the new gallery in his birthplace of Edinburgh, which opened in 1999.

In the '80s and '90s, a modern school of Glasgow Boys emerged, such as Stephen Campbell, Stephen Conroy, Peter Howson, Ken Currie and others who have become worthy successors to the original Glasgow Boys. The most talked-about Scottish artist in the late 1990s has been a woman who has produced less than flattering images of her own gender; in doing so, Jenny Saville has managed to achieve both award-winning critical and popular acclaim.

It is perhaps the greatest achievement of Scotland's artists in the twentieth century that their work is now widely viewed, debated and taken seriously, even in Scotland.

'What do you mean, there's a resemblance?' Former Lord Provost of Glasgow Pat Lally in front of a work by modern 'Glasgow Boy' Peter Howson

MUSIC AND DANCE

It took until the 1960s for Scotland to get itself fully fledged national opera and ballet companies, though these two art forms had begun to flourish much earlier. In the case of the former, however, it was left largely to touring companies and home-based amateur groups to carry opera's flag in the first half of the century.

Scottish Opera was largely the brainchild of Scottish music's most influential figure, the late Sir Alexander Gibson. From 1959, under his leadership, the Royal Scottish National Orchestra was arguably Scotland's greatest single cultural institution. With demand for opera on the increase, in 1962 he and several visionary musicians and music-lovers in Glasgow created Scottish Opera, based at first in the city's King's Theatre before taking over the Theatre Royal as its headquarters in 1974.

Sir Alexander Gibson in full flow

Scottish Opera has not had its troubles to seek

After years of financial crisis, the opera company is merging with its Glasgow neighbour Scottish Ballet, itself founded as recently as 1968 when the Scottish Arts Council invited Western Theatre Ballet to move to Glasgow from Bristol – a previous attempt to establish a Scottish National Ballet had foundered within a year of its foundation in 1960. Initially named the Scottish Theatre Ballet, the new company at first enjoyed success and produced great dancers such as Elaine McDonald and memorable productions such as *The Nutcracker*. Renamed Scottish Ballet in 1974, in the 1990s the company underwent a series of financial and administrative crises which culminated in the effective dismissal of its board by the Scottish Arts Council and the enforced merger with Scottish Opera.

Other dance forms have been ignored by comparison with the national ballet company, but a new national Dancebase is presently under construction in Edinburgh and, certainly, highland dancing continues to flourish.

In classical music, as well as the national orchestra, Scotland now has the Scottish Chamber Orchestra and the BBC Scottish Symphony Orchestra, which was the first full-time permanent orchestra in Scotland when it was founded in 1935. Scotland has also produced its fair share of clas-

sical musicians and composers in the twentieth century, but, as with other art forms, they have often
enjoyed more acclaim abroad. An exception to that
rule is Evelyn Glennie, the percussionist who over-
came deafness to become a world leader in her spe-
cialism, and composers such as Thea Musgrave,
Robin Orr and latterly James MacMillan have produced operas and other orchestral pieces which are
already standard works.

Three great individual Scottish singers found
worldwide fame on the operatic stage. First, Mary
Garden (1877–1967) was a strong-willed soprano
who was reported to have been the lover of Claude

Although the late Margot
Fonteyn is no longer with
us, Scottish Ballet . . .

Debussy. She took leading roles in the world's great opera houses from 1900 to
1931, becoming director of the Chicago Grand Opera in the process, before retiring to her native Aberdeen. Second, the talents of Edinburgh-born Joseph Hislop
(1884–1977) were discovered while he was working in Sweden, where he rose to
become leading tenor in the Royal Swedish Opera before his international career
took off. The composer Puccini, no less, described him as his ideal leading tenor.
He later became a renowned singing teacher and one of his pupils was the leading Scottish baritone Donald Maxwell. Third, David Ward (1922–83), born in
Dumbarton, was one of the world's great bass singers and practically made his
own the role of Wotan in Wagner's *Ring*. Since the establishment of Scottish
Opera, Scotland has produced a string of highly rated individual performers such
as sopranos Linda Esther Gray and Isobel Buchanan.

. . . and Scottish Opera will
merge to live on

Scotland's orchestras enjoy
a high reputation abroad

THE POPS IN THEATRE AND MUSIC

In so-called popular culture, Scotland has made an international impact through its comedians and musicians. Music hall and 'variety' dominated theatrical life in Scotland for decades. The four cities and many towns had their own theatres, and a Scottish circuit developed from the Gaiety in Ayr to Her Majesty's in Aberdeen, while in Edinburgh and Glasgow it seemed as if musical theatre would never die – in 1959 more than 450,000 people saw the *Half Past Eight* revue in its summer run at the Glasgow Alhambra. Over the years all the major British and American stars visited Scotland; the Empire Theatre in Glasgow became notorious as the graveyard of English comedians, but it also gave Jerry Lewis and Dean Martin some of their finest hours.

Scottish music hall produced such giants as Sir Harry Lauder and the comedians Will Fyffe, Tommy Morgan, Harry Gordon and Dave Willis. Robert Wilson, billed as the voice of Scotland, started a line of Scottish singers-in-tartan that continued with varying degrees of talent through Kenneth McKellar, the Alexander Brothers, Andy Stewart and Peter Morrison, while Sidney Devine's success as a country singer and sex symbol was one of the more inexplicable phenomena of recent years. Though largely retired, Stanley Baxter, Jimmy Logan and Rikki Fulton are great actors and performers who kept alive the Scottish tradition of pantomime – the last remaining link with the great days of Scottish musical theatre – assisted by the likes of Jack Milroy, Russell Hunter, Una McLean, Gerard Kelly and Allan Stewart. The surreal genius of Chic Murray was perhaps the last great product of variety in Scotland.

In the era of rock and pop music, Scotland has produced many fine individual artists and bands who have enjoyed worldwide success. In the 1950s, Lonnie

Will Fyffe was rightly honoured after his retirement

Stanley Baxter, the grandest of dames

Chic Murray – genius

Rikki Fulton as the Revd I.M. Jolly

The Big Yin wears a big yin

Donegan pioneered the craze for back-to-basics skiffle music, and in the 1960s Marie Lawrie from Glasgow became one of Britain's biggest stars under her stage name of Lulu. The 1970s brought the most astonishing Scottish pop phenomenon of them all – the Bay City Rollers. It is estimated that these four tartan-clad lads sold more than 50 million records, but they split up amid some acrimony in 1982.

In the post-punk era, Simple Minds were the country's leading rock band, while Aberdeen-born Annie Lennox became Scotland's biggest-selling female artist, firstly as part of Eurythmics and then as a solo singer. Bands such as Big Country, Deacon Blue, Texas and the Proclaimers enjoyed a string of hits in the

The Corries, leaders of the folk revival who made 'Flower of Scotland' the people's anthem

Lonnie Donegan – have briefcase, will skiffle

Lulu, still going strong

So we sang shang-a-lang . . .

. . . and we Rolled with the gang

'80s and '90s, while Clydebank's Wet Wet Wet were the biggest-selling Scottish band of the 1990s. Early 1999 saw the emergence of Scots-born Shirley Manson, lead singer of American band Garbage, as a major star.

Folk music and dance also underwent a revival in the second half of the century. The poet and writer Hamish Henderson organised the People's Festival Ceilidhs as well as ensuring the collection of much oral material and songs. In Glasgow, the folk scene attracted many talented performers such as Euan McColl, Hamish Imlach and Matt McGinn, with the Labour politicians Norman and Janey Buchan invariably at the centre of organising events. The greatest individual product of that scene in the '60s and '70s was a man with long hair, welly boots and a unique brand of humour. Billy Connolly made the leap from Glasgow folk-club singer to international star and has proved his talent as an actor, most notably in the film *Mrs Brown*.

Popular music through the ages has always been accompanied by dance, and at one time Glasgow alone boasted 13 large dance halls, with ballroom dancing the dominant form for decades. The disco years followed but have themselves given way to clubs and raves which now co-exist peacefully with ceilidhs, which, though somewhat more frenetic than in yesteryear, have been successfully revived in the 1990s as part of the resurgence in the folk scene.

Who needs a ballroom to dance?

BROADCASTING AND THE SCREEN

Scotland does not yet have a film industry in many people's eyes, as the country has no major studios, though plans are under way for at least four such studios. Sean Connery, the Edinburgh milkman who became James Bond, is by far the biggest film star Scotland has produced and is arguably the most famous Scotsman on the planet. Only in the latter part of his career have his talents as an actor been truly appreciated, and although resident abroad he remains a proud patriot known for his support of the Scottish National Party.

Scotland has always had a presence on the screen, most often as the location for films, which is still the country's main contribution to the industry. It can also be seen as the birthplace of one kind of film – the 'father of documentaries' was the name rightly given to the director John Grierson. He was one of the moving forces behind Films of Scotland, the state-funded body which enjoyed an extraordinary output of more than 150 mostly business-orientated short films in the 1950s and '60s under the dynamic leadership of former *Scotsman* journalist Forsyth Hardy, who was also a leading light in the establishment of the Edinburgh Film Festival. Grierson achieved recognition elsewhere, becoming the founding director of the National Film Board of Canada.

Scotland in the past was, it appears, too small to support an indigenous industry of any size. That is not to say, however, that Scotland has not produced its fair share of film actors, directors, writers and technicians. Stan Laurel first started in showbusiness while living in Glasgow, where his father was a theatre manager, and he and Oliver Hardy visited Scotland on several occasions after they reached stardom. Character actors such as Finlay Currie, James Robertson Justice, Beryl Reid and many more were all leading players on screen. Prior to Connery, Scotland's greatest leading man of film was David Niven, the former Highland Light Infantry officer who became the quintessential Englishman, just as the archetypal English rose was Helensburgh-born Deborah Kerr.

In the modern era, actors such as Tom Conti, Bill Paterson, Brian Cox and Ian Bannen, killed in a car crash in 1999, proved their worth in lead and character roles, while the 1990s crop of acting talent features Robert Carlyle, Dougray Scott, Alan Cummings, Robbie Coltrane, Kelly MacDonald and Ewan McGregor, presently the country's biggest star. Producers and directors such as James Lee, Bill Forsyth, Michael Caton-Jones, Douglas Eadie and

All the stars came here. Trigger even brought Roy Rogers . . .

. . . while Mr Laurel brought Mr Hardy to see his old home town of Glasgow

An extremely rare picture of Sean Connery as a soldierly extra in a show at the King's Theatre, Edinburgh

Charles Gormley have been major forces behind the camera. Writers such as Danny Boyle, Alan Sharpe and Allan Scott, the pen name of Allan Shiach, have all written on distinctive Scottish themes as well as international subjects.

In broadcasting, from the outset the BBC has had a separate Scottish dimension at the insistence of the corporation's founding father, the domineering Scot Lord Reith, though he later presided over the 'metropolisation' of BBC services to make them more London-based. For many years the BBC operated only on radio, and the corporation's Scottish headquarters in Glasgow maintained a steady output, becoming the first BBC station to broadcast a complete play, *Rob Roy*, as early as 1923. The corporation has always responded to challenges, such as the advent of successful commercial stations like Radio Clyde and Radio Forth in the 1970s. BBC Radio Scotland came to life as the only station covering the whole country. The deregulation of radio means that the corporation now has commercial competition in most areas.

How to make a broadcaster run away and leave you

BBC television in Scotland faced its greatest challenge in 1955 when Scottish Television was founded, broadcasting from Glasgow, to be followed six years later by Grampian and Borders Television. From the outset, Scottish Television's output was couthy and populist, and shows like *The One O'Clock Gang* and *The White Heather Club* made stars of performers like Andy Stewart and Larry Marshall. Late in life, John Grierson found a new career as presenter of nature series *This Wonderful World*.

A seminal drama for STV, as it used to be known, was Jeremy

The original crew of the
Vital Spark, perhaps BBC
Scotland's most fondly
remembered series

Isaacs' production of *A Sense of Freedom*, based on Jimmy Boyle's life story. The talents which gathered at Cowcaddens for this film stayed to work on *Taggart* and (*Take the*) *High Road*, the station's two long-running series for the ITV network. Meanwhile, classic television series such as *Dr Finlay's Casebook*, *Sutherland's Law* and especially *Sunset Song* and *Tutti Frutti* proved that BBC Scotland could more than match the rest of the BBC network for drama. Sports and news broadcasting has always been a strength of both the main channels and BBC Scotland pioneered the use of 'on air' news input from different studios in the 1960s.

Both terrestrial broadcasters have recently faced the challenge of satellite television, which at first largely ignored Scotland as a separate entity but which now broadcasts more live Scottish football, for instance, than STV and BBC put together.

Independent producers have become an established and successful part of the television scene in Scotland since the industry was largely deregulated under the Thatcher government. Further deregulation could yet significantly affect commerical television in Scotland, however. The merger of Scottish Television and Grampian Television as part of the Scottish Media Group may not be sufficient to stop its takeover by non-Scottish interests.

THEATRE

In the early 1900s J.M. Barrie was Scotland's best-known playwright, and his plays such as *Peter Pan* and *The Admirable Crichton* were destined for massive success on the English stage. In Scotland, however, he was perhaps better known as the author of several works of the kailyard school of fiction.

The first real step towards a revival of serious theatre in Scotland took place in 1908 when the Glasgow Repertory Company was founded, inspired by the Abbey Theatre in Dublin, by then already considered to be Ireland's national theatre. Attempts to start a similar national theatre for Scotland and the continuing debate about whether such a theatre should be established have surfaced in Scotland throughout the twentieth century.

The Glasgow Rep folded in 1914, but after the First World War the St Andrew's Society in Glasgow established the Scottish National Players, which, under the guidance of Sir Tyrone Guthrie, lasted from 1921 to 1936. Its declared aim was to promote drama dealing with Scotland, and as such it could be seen as the first national theatre. It was the first company to produce the work of James Bridie (Dr Osborne Henry Mavor) and had the support of the Scottish National Theatre Society, which was formed in 1922 but ended in 1939 following the outbreak of the Second World War.

During the war, Bridie established the Citizens' Theatre company which took over the Princess's Theatre in the Gorbals, where it is based to this day. The Citizens' is not the oldest repertory company in Scotland, however – that honour belongs to Perth, established in 1935, followed by Dundee Rep and the Byre Theatre in St Andrews, both founded in 1939.

After the war the Unity Players in Glasgow produced ground-breaking drama such as *The Gorbals Story* and Ena Lamont's *Men Should Weep*, which has been successfully revived several times since. The Unity Players folded through lack of funds in 1951 but by then the Citizens' Theatre was on its way to becoming Scotland's leading company. The first major Scottish contribution to the Edinburgh Festival came at the second festival in 1948, when Sir Tyrone Guthrie and the Citizens' mounted a breathtaking production of *Ane Satyre of the Thrie Estaitis*, the 400-year-old play by Sir David Lyndsay. At that time the Citizens' was the place for talented Scottish actors such as Duncan Macrae, Fulton Mackay, Roddy Macmillan and Stanley Baxter. It would later become Scotland's best-known company under the direction of Giles Havergal, Philip Prowse and Robert David Macdonald, whose policy of presenting international works in new and dynamic versions confirmed the Citizens' reputation.

The '50s were something of a golden era for Scottish drama, with the establishment of the drama school in Glasgow, now part of the Royal Scottish Academy of Music and Drama, the foundation of the Pitlochry Festival Theatre and the setting-up of the Gateway Theatre in Edinburgh, where Robert Kemp's plays were produced and where actors such as Tom Fleming, later to become broadcasting's voice for state occasions, first started. In the 1980s Fleming attempted to kick-start the national theatre with his touring Scottish Theatre Company, but it also failed financially despite the success of productions such as

Scottish theatre has never
been afraid to take risks

Kemp's *Let Wives Tak Tent*.

The Gateway lasted until 1965, when the Edinburgh Civic Theatre started in the Royal Lyceum, whose name the company later adopted. It was in the Lyceum in the 1970s that the company, led by Greenock playwright and director Bill Bryden, almost became the Scottish National Theatre. The director's own play *Willie Rough* was a high point of the Lyceum's productions, and he later went on to become director of the National Theatre in London before returning to Glasgow with his own major productions such as *The Ship* and *The Big Picnic*. Although it faced financial difficulties for many years, the Lyceum company continues to produce varied works under director Kenny Ireland.

The Traverse Theatre is now housed in a purpose-built complex adjoining the Usher Hall and the Lyceum. It began in 1963 in cramped quarters in Edinburgh's Grassmarket, and its brave policy of presenting new writing continues to this day.

From the 1960s to the present day, Scotland has seen a large number of touring companies presenting many works of varying quality. Chief among them have been the 7:84 company, the musical Wildcat Theatre, the innovative Borderline company and Communicado, whose production of Edwin Morgan's translation of *Cyrano de Bergerac* provided a highlight for Scottish theatre, only for the company to be riven by internal dissent. The collapse of Glasgow's cultural festival Mayfest in 1997 deprived many of the smaller companies such as Theatre About Glasgow of a regular engagement, and despite the National Lottery awards, many Scottish theatres and theatre companies have struggled financially in recent years, though new companies such as Raindog have proved that there is a demand for such companies. Certainly, there is no shortage of community-based amateur dramatic and musical companies across Scotland.

Given the Lottery investment in theatre buildings, it is fair to say that Scotland now has plenty of theatres but not enough companies or investment in productions to fill them. There is, however, no shortage of Scottish material for such companies. Numerous Scottish playwrights have emerged in the past three decades, and such writers as C.P. Taylor, Tom McGrath, Liz Lochhead, Hector MacMillan, John Byrne, John McGrath, Chris Hannan, David Greig and Sharman MacDonald have produced works which, along with those of Bridie and Kemp, would provide the basic Scottish repertoire for any National Theatre of Scotland.

INDUSTRY, COMMERCE, INNOVATORS AND ENTREPRENEURS

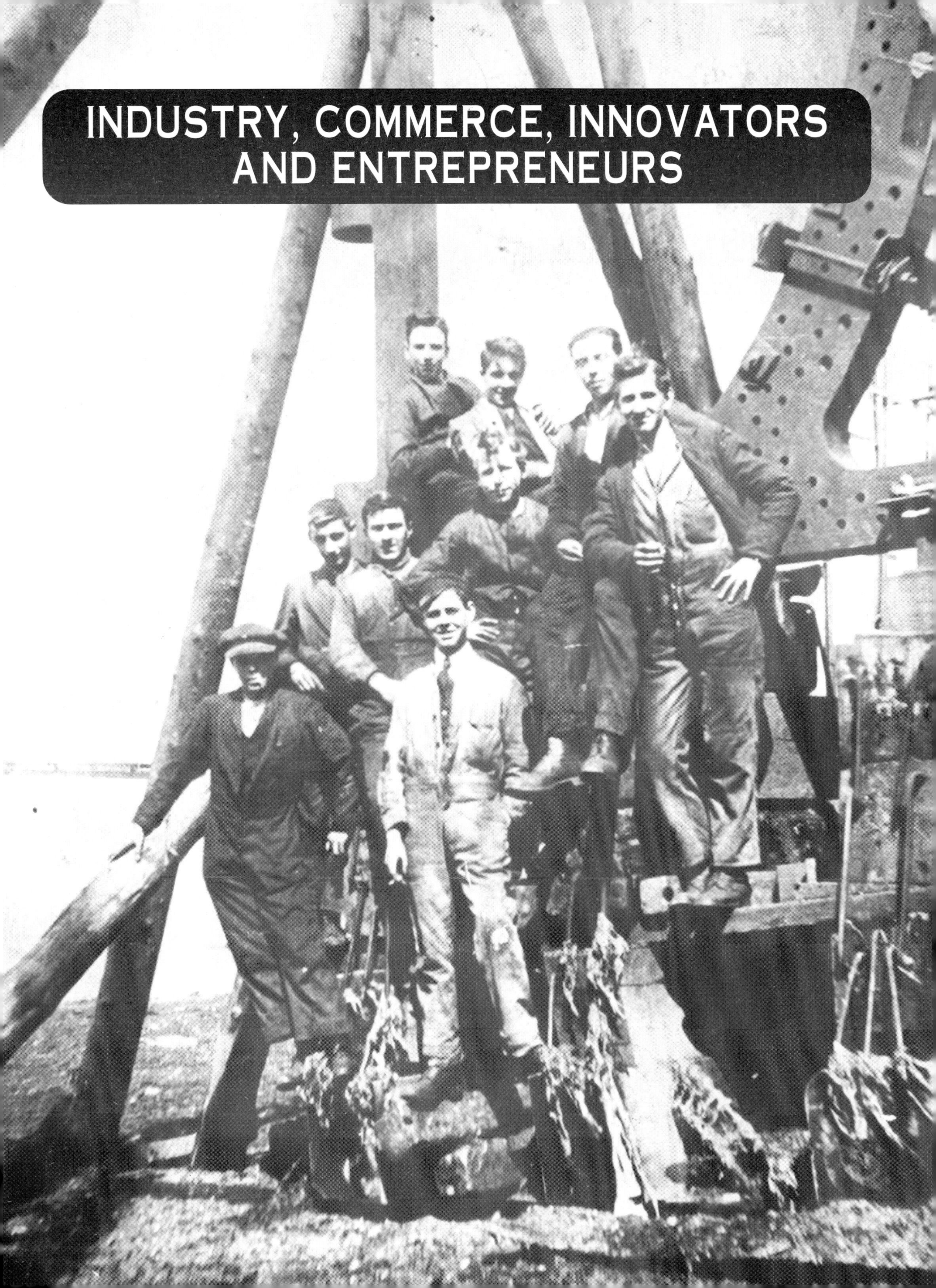

In this brief examination we highlight significant people and trends in the development of Scottish business and industry during the twentieth century.

INDUSTRY

The massive expansion of manufacturing industry in Scotland in the Victorian era continued in the early part of the twentieth century, but many major industries have declined since the Second World War and some, such as coal mining and steel manufacture, have all but disappeared.

Shipbuilding is the best-known example of a failed world-leading Scottish industry. It was Scotland's biggest industry in terms of output for most of the century, and even in the 1950s one third of all new British shipping was made in Scotland. The early part of the 1900s saw Clydeside's greatest days, when Scottish shipbuilding was at its peak. There were great yards in Leith and Aberdeen and on Tayside, but 'Clyde-built' was the byword for shipbuilding in those days. Beardmore's giant forge – Europe's largest – in the east end of Glasgow and many other iron and steel foundries provided the raw material for the yards.

Technical innovations, particularly in marine engineering, gave Clydeside a world lead – from 1900 to 1910 it was estimated that a third of the world's new ships were launched on the Clyde. As early as December 1907, however, the shipbuilding companies had protested to the government about the Japanese subsidising their industry and undercutting British yards. Although the war provided a brief surge, by the 1920s a massive slump in orders had seen some yards close

Beardmore's forge in Parkhead, Glasgow, now the site of a shopping centre

Apprentices learned 'a trade for life'. Or perhaps not

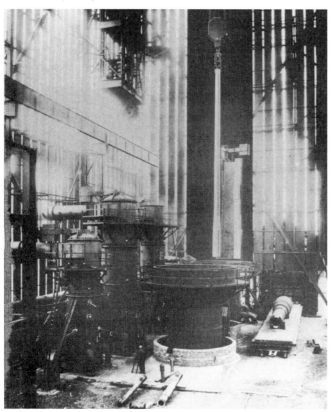

The launch of the Clyde's last ocean-going paddle steamer, the PS *Waverley*

Welding replaced riveting as the 'glue' of ships built on the Clyde

and others amalgamate, while others closed from 1929 onwards under a national shipbuilding strategy.

Many steelmakers and shipbuilders had formed alliances, and the collapse of one industry had its effect on the other. The 1930s' Depression provided a stark example of shipbuilding's problems. In 1931, work ceased on the hull of a giant liner then known simply as No. 534 at John Brown's yard, where thousands were promptly laid off. But with government help, and symbolic of a national revival, Cunard began work again on the ship and on 26 September 1934 the *Queen Mary* was launched, to be followed four years and a day later by the *Queen Elizabeth*. Both ships dominated Atlantic crossings for a period after the war, but the former is now a tourist attraction at Long Beach, California, while the latter was converted into a floating university before being destroyed by fire in Hong Kong harbour in 1972.

The Second World War saw a revival of shipbuilding, and afterwards there was increased demand for ships to replace those sunk during the hostilities. This also boosted other industries such as steel manufacture. It was a heady period which only confirmed the dominance of labour-intensive heavy industry in Scotland –

The *Queen Elizabeth II* settles in the Clyde
shortly after her launch

The men of Upper Clyde Shipbuilders vote
for action

which in turn made the periods of recession so devastating.

Increased competition from yards elsewhere,
often subsidised, wrought havoc on Scottish shipbuilding, and in the 1960s the crisis reached a peak.
Closures were threatened on an almost monthly
basis, though the Clyde had one last great hurrah
with the launch of the *Queen Elizabeth II* on 20
September 1967 at John Brown's in Clydebank. The
following year the Labour government intervened
after the Geddes Committee recommended the
amalgamation of the remaining yards into Upper
Clyde Shipbuilders, which in turn was liquidated in
1971, forcing the famous workers' sit-in and eventual u-turn and assistance from the Conservative

Mining supported and
involved whole communities
in the early 1900s

government. The 1980s' recession all but killed off shipbuilding in Scotland, with
Aberdeen, Leith and Dundee's yards closing. On the Clyde, Yarrow's still produces warships, while Govan Shipbuilders' survival hangs by a thread.

Shipbuilding's decline was mirrored in other heavy industries. Coal mining
employed 15 per cent of the male population at the turn of the century but the
number of pits was already in decline by the Depression of the 1930s, which
accelerated the process. Nationalisation of the industry after the war failed to
prevent further decline and job loss and more than 110 pits closed, nearly all
because their reserves were exhausted, in the ten years up to 1967. The introduction of so-called 'superpits' such as Bilston Glen in Midlothian had only a
temporary relief effect. The long miners' strike of 1984–85 was the last major
battle of a century punctuated by industrial strife and in the end the entire industry lost. Afterwards the number of pits declined to single figures until now the
Longannet complex is left as the last deep mine in Scotland.

Government intervention to support industry had already begun before the
Second World War and the growth of Special Development Areas saw industrial
estates spring up throughout Scotland in the '50s and '60s. In the Highlands, the
North of Scotland Hydro Board brought major changes with its promise of cheap
power. Foreign investment, particularly from America, saw such names as
Honeywell, Caterpillar and IBM appear on the Scottish scene, paving the way for
later multi-national investment.

In 1957, a new steel strip mill was opened at government insistence by
Colville's at Ravenscraig near Motherwell, despite doubts about its viability. It
became a totem in Scottish industry.

The 1960s saw massive state-sponsored investment in Scotland. An attempt to
create a car manufacturing industry began with Rootes at Linwood and BMC, later
British Leyland, at Bathgate. The Highland and Islands Development Board was set
up in 1965 to tackle depopulation in the Highlands and they brought major investment in an aluminium smelter at Invergordon and a pulp mill at Corpach.

Increasing unemployment saw more government intervention in the 1970s,
with the Scottish Development Agency, later Scottish Enterprise, having an

Elementary cleaning for a 1950s miner

A sight almost gone from Scotland – miners pose in front of their colliery's winding gear

Opposite: Ravenscraig shortly before the end

investment budget of £500 million at its peak. Traditional industries continued to decline and the cities were particularly badly affected. Dundee, the city of jute, jam and journalism, now has just the last.

Other strong Scottish industries have suffered. The concentration of ownership in whisky distilling has closed many small distilleries and even large bottling plants. The worst-ever blow to Scotland's newspaper industry was in 1974 when the Beaverbrook group pulled out of Glasgow with the loss of 1,700 jobs.

Yet there have been periods of recovery. In the past quarter-century Scotland has virtually created two major industries from scratch. North Sea oil was first piped ashore in 1975, and the need for rigs and workers to drill for oil gave Scottish industry an immense boost. The '80s then saw the growth of the electronic industry, creating a silicon glen to not quite rival California's Silicon Valley, and by 1990 almost half of Scottish manufacturing exports were in this sector. The industry is almost wholly owned abroad, however, and is vulnerable to recession elsewhere, as the mothballing of the giant Korean-owned Hyundai semiconductor plant near Dunfermline proved in 1998.

Heavy industry is almost a thing of the past . . .

. . . as much as these jute mills in Dundee

An industry was built from scratch, as here in Methil, Fife, but how long before the oil runs out?

The 1980s and 1990s saw the virtual collapse of heavy manufacturing in Scotland. Those expensive investments at Linwood, Bathgate, Corpach and Invergordon all failed as the Tory government refused state intervention in failing industries. So inured had Scotland become to bad news in heavy manufacturing that the closure of Ravenscraig by British Steel in 1992 provoked more sorrow than anger.

Successful Scottish industries have also been subjected to takeovers from abroad. The mighty Distillers company was taken over by Guinness in hugely controversial circumstances after a protracted battle in the 1980s. But the 'Scottish card' has been successfully used to defend Scottish business, such as when Scottish and Newcastle fought off a hostile 'raid' from Australian giant Elder's.

The most successful industries in terms of increase in wealth generation have been tourism, insurance and banking; tourism is now Scotland's largest industry in terms of people employed. With a few exceptions, and despite recent corporate raids, Scotland's financial-services sector has also managed to stave off foreign and English-based competitors who have enviously eyed the Scottish banks and insurance companies' deservedly high reputations and earnings. Edinburgh-based Standard Life, for instance, remains one of the largest mutual companies in the world.

The best example of the upsurge in banking fortunes has been the changes experienced in recent years by the Bank and the Royal Bank of Scotland. In the 1980s and early 1990s, both were seen as ripe for takeover and the Standard Chartered Bank came close to acquiring the Bank of Scotland. In October 1999, the Bank of Scotland launched an audacious £22 billion bid to take over the larger London-based NatWest bank. Its main competitor in the NatWest contest was its near neighbour the Royal Bank of Scotland.

Corpach, in the shadow of Ben Nevis, where a pulp-mill industry was born, lived and died inside 30 years

The traditions of Scottish banks included the Bank of Scotland's annual boardroom picture

Early aviator Preston Watson in flight near Dundee. Some say he may even have beaten the Wright brothers into the air

INNOVATORS AND ENTREPRENEURS

Scotland is rightly proud of its many inventors and the twentieth century has seen continuing innovation and development both in Scotland and by Scots working further afield. It is difficult to single out inventions from a long list, but two which changed the world were radar and television.

Sir Robert Watson-Watt, born in Brechin in 1892, did not actually invent radar by himself, and he never claimed to have been a sole pioneer. What he did achieve was the plan for the first working system for radio detection and ranging, which was the difference between success and failure in the Battle of Britain. Watson-Watt was knighted and awarded £52,000 by the government for his work. He died in 1973.

On 26 January 1926, the first working demonstration of real television in public was made by John Logie Baird to members of the Royal Institute in his workshop in London. Baird was a pioneer of electronics, and his system for storing images underpins all modern video technology. Worn out by war work, some of which is still secret, he died in 1946 at the age of 58.

The two men had something in common: they were unable to take commercial advantage of their inventions. This has often led to the accusation that Scottish industry lacks real entrepreneurial spirit, but Scotland has always had its fair share of entrepreneurs. Before the start of the twentieth century, Scotland had already provided America with two of its greatest industrial figures.

Andrew Carnegie

Alexander Graham Bell mobbed by schoolboys on a trip to his home city of
Edinburgh

Brian Souter and his sister Anne Gloag

On 11 August 1919, Andrew Carnegie, once the world's richest man, died at his home in Massachusetts at the age of 83. He
was born in Dunfermline but his family emigrated to
Pennsylvania in 1848. Though small in stature, he became a giant
of industry, dominating the iron and steel sector in America in the
late 1800s. In 1900 he began to systematically give away much of
his fortune, endowing libraries across the world. His generosity to
his native land, where he bought and developed Skibo Castle in
Sutherland as a holiday home, can be seen in libraries and universities around the country.

In 1920, in a famous return to his home country, Alexander
Graham Bell was mobbed by schoolchildren during a brief visit to
his birthplace of Edinburgh. The inventor of the telephone had
emigrated to Canada in 1870 but retained great affection for his
homeland. He died in 1922.

In the latter part of the twentieth century, Scotland saw the rise of a new breed of entrepreneur. Lord MacFarlane of Bearsden built a packaging business virtually from scratch before rescuing the tarnished name of Guinness after the Distillers takeover. David Murray built his steel stockholding business into an international concern that includes Rangers Football Club, while Tom Hunter developed his Sports Division into a massive business before selling it. Sir Tom Farmer started business with a small garage and built the Kwik Fit empire before selling it to Ford for a reputed £1 billion in 1999. Brother and sister Brian Souter and Anne Gloag are Scotland's richest people, having built the international Stagecoach transport empire from scratch. They still operate from their original headquarters in Perth, and they exemplify the modern Scottish entrepreneurial spirit which sees Scotland's location not as a hindrance but as a good place from which to do business.

SOCIAL HISTORY

If Scotland's population growth had kept pace with that of England during the twentieth century, there would now be more than 6.5 million people resident north of the border, instead of just 5 million.

The phenomenon of Scotland's missing population has intrigued sociologists for decades, yet the reasons are simple. Poverty and lack of opportunities across Scotland saw many more people emigrate than came here, and the declining birth rate in the latter part of the century has exacerbated the trend – in the last two decades the population has continued to fall, and it is down 200,000 from the 1971 census figure.

Emigration was a fact of life in many parts of Scotland in the twentieth century. It reached a peak in the 1920s, with almost 400,000 people leaving the country, but the trend continued into the '50s and '60s, when 500,000 people left.

By contrast, immigration has tended to come in waves, bringing the so-called New Scots into the country in numbers that have never threatened to replace those who have left. The mass Irish immigration of the nineteenth century continued into the twentieth, and was not welcome in many quarters. As late as 1923, the General Assembly of the Church of Scotland published a notorious paper on the threat Catholic Irish immigration posed to 'our Scottish nationality' and called for limits on immigration.

Jews, Italians, Lithuanians and other Europeans came to Scotland, including conspicuous French vegetable-sellers known as Onion Johnnies. Asian immigra-

Children from a travelling family in the early years of the century

tion was almost entirely concentrated in the second half of the century and, though hardly immigrants in a United Kingdom, English people have also come to live in Scotland in sizeable numbers.

Immigration from both Catholic and Protestant persuasions in Ireland led to the most serious religious problem of the century – apart, that is, from the sheer decline in the practice of religion. Sectarianism has never been a strictly religious issue, as politics and economics are equally involved, but there is no doubt that Scotland was split along religious lines in the early part of the century. From 1916 onwards Catholic communities in the central belt supported the IRA both tacitly and openly, while the Orange Order grew in strength and influence in proportion to fears over Catholic infiltration of Protestant communities and workplaces.

The 1930s saw the peak of sectarianism in Scotland when, in one municipal election in Glasgow, anti-Catholic candidates polled more votes than Labour. Ironically, both world wars assisted the assimilation of Catholics into the Scottish population as religious differences were set aside to combat the common enemy.

That sectarianism is on the wane cannot be doubted, and those totems of the divide, Rangers and Celtic, have themselves both played their part in recent years in attempting to dispel bigotry. In

Three orphans pictured in Glasgow in 1903 shortly after they were found and before they were taken to an orphanage

Many people recall seeing Onion Johnnies, but how many were there in Scotland?

Judging by statistics alone, Christianity is but a shadow of its former self, yet the various churches still wield enormous influence over many lives

Mick McGahey, the late trade-union leader, at the end of a century in which working-class struggles were a feature for so long

Scots were prominent among the Orange marchers at the showdown at Drumcree in Northern Ireland, yet Ulster's sectarian troubles have largely not been imported to Scotland

Pope John Paul II with Cardinal Gordon Joseph Gray during his historic visit to Scotland in 1982

A typical scene in a
communal washhouse
where many women spent
much of their lives

1982, perhaps the greatest symbol of religious tolerance came when Pope John
Paul II visited Scotland and was greeted in the shadow of John Knox's statue by
the Moderator of the General Assembly of the Church of Scotland.

    The decline in the practice of religion has been a trend since the 1930s, though
Catholic Mass attendance reached a peak in the 1970s before it, too, began to
fall rapidly. For the Church of Scotland and the smaller Presbyterian churches,

most of the twentieth century has been a story of declining attendances and reducing income.

Scotland is now a much more secular country than it was in 1900, and improved education and the reduction of the heavy industries have meant a change in class distinction for many people. Few young Scots would now describe themselves as – or even understand what is meant by – traditional working class.

The position of women in society has also changed dramatically throughout the century. Female emancipation was fought for in Scotland just as fiercely as in England, and from a position in the 1920s where the greatest number of women workers were to be found in domestic service, women slowly made their way into many more professions, often overcoming sex segregation to do so. In October 1999 it was announced that, for the first time, women made up more than half of the Scottish workforce. However, although pay inequalities and discrimination on gender grounds were supposed to have been outlawed in the 1970s, these still continue in many areas of industry and commerce.

The call centre of its day – an early Post Office telephone exchange where women were almost exclusively preferred to men

It is not just in the workplace that women's position in society has changed. The increase in divorce and cohabitation has also contributed to the increase in the proportion of single women within the population.

For all Scots, including women, the twentieth century has seen fundamental changes in the individual's relationship with the state. The monarchy and the political establishment no longer preside over automatic subservience by the mass of the populace, with Scots more questioning and better informed about the activities of the state than ever before.

Certainly, Scotland has not been averse to showing off its confidence. The great exhibitions in Glasgow and Edinburgh in 1901 and 1908, followed by Glasgow's Empire Exhibition in 1938, were remarkable displays that showed Scotland to the world and the world to Scotland. In recent years Glasgow has deliberately looked to their example to renew itself, with the 1988 Garden

A corporation tram shows how the monarchy was revered at the time of King George V's coronation in 1910

Opposite: The helter-skelter at the Scottish National Exhibition in Saughton Park, Edinburgh, in 1908

Festival, the Year of Culture in 1990 – in attendance terms, Scotland's largest public festival of the century – and the 1999 Year of Architecture and Design all showing municipal confidence.

The other cities have had their moments too. Aberdeen was dubbed the oil capital of Europe after the North Sea explorations discovered oil and gas, Dundee has re-invented itself as the City of Discovery after a long regeneration programme, and Edinburgh's revival was crowned in 1992 when the city hosted the European Summit.

Most Scottish towns and villages retain strong community loyalties and the many traditional local festivals and events such as Common Ridings have been added to by some 'instant traditions' such as gala queens and sports days.

As communities have changed, so too has society as a whole. At the turn of the century, property ownership was confined to the upper middle class and the aristocracy. Scottish housing was, in the main, quite appalling. There may be those who hark back to tenement life in the cities as a golden age, but the truth is that overcrowding and disease were rife. The Second World War provided the

The old-fashioned way of
celebrating Hogmanay . . .

impetus to change Scotland's housing stock for ever. In two decades from 1945, almost 600,000 new homes were built in Scotland, most of them council housing. The population of Glasgow in particular was 'overspilled' into surrounding areas, and this policy, along with the building of the New Towns, represents the largest exercise in social engineering of the twentieth century. But at the time the Thatcher government took power in 1979, the majority of Scots still did not own their homes. The Conservative and now Labour right-to-buy policies have transformed that situation, as has the availability of cheaper mortgages, so that home ownership now far exceeds the renting of accommodation. In addition, much of the public-sector housing has been transferred to housing associations rather than councils.

Scottish people have also broadened their horizons. Like people in every other Western country, they have taken advantage of cheap travel to holiday abroad.

. . . has given way to the new-fangled Edinburgh's Hogmanay Festival. There's still the same enjoyment, but many more people having a good time

Eviction was once a common sight in Scottish housing estates

There were days when the boats at the Clyde jetties couldn't fill up fast enough to go 'Doon the Watter'

The traditional 'Doon the Watter' holiday enjoyed by Glaswegians for much of the twentieth century is now all but gone, with only one paddle steamer, the *Waverley*, still operating on the Clyde.

Scots are also much more fashion conscious than in the days of the flappers, utility clothing and the swinging '60s. Glasgow is a leading fashion centre in Britain and in all the cities and many towns smart restaurants and bars have opened, reflecting greater knowledge about food and increased leisure time and disposable income enjoyed by many people.

Some Scottish concerns are much more than fashionable fads. There is now greater awareness over issues such as transport and the environment than at any other point in the century; people are aware, for instance, that the huge increase in car ownership has had its downside in the shape of increased pollution. Scottish society has changed beyond all recognition in the past 100 years. For most Scots, the conclusion has to be that the changes have been for the better.

The Duke of Buccleuch, the owner of Scotland's largest private estates, pictured with the Duchess in the 1950s

The building of the Carbeth huts which have been at the centre of a bitter dispute over land ownership in recent years

One issue has dominated the history of rural Scotland in the twentieth century, as it did in previous centuries. Ownership of land is still the thorniest issue of all to those who live on the land. Agitation for land reform has seen many high-profile and often bitter arguments over ownership. Famous cases include the various 'seizures' of land by tenants, and latterly the most famous ownership case was the eventual purchase in 1998 of their island by the people of Eigg after years of battling against insensitive owners.

Land reform and the ending of feudalism will be the first major issue to be tackled by the Scottish Parliament in the new century, some 130 years after the first serious political agitation for reform brought about, among other things, the Crofters' Party and the Crofting Act of 1886. Though dramatically reduced throughout the twentieth century, crofting is still a way of life for some people in parts of the Highlands and islands, but it is under continuing threat, both from depopulation and from incoming migrants buying land and houses for speculative purposes or as holiday homes.

Depopulation of rural areas has been a feature of the twentieth century. The most symbolic of many migrations was the extinction of an entire way of life on 29 August 1930, when the people of the St Kilda archipelago were taken, at their own request, to the mainland. St Kilda had once supported several hundred

Grouse moors are a blot on the landscape, say some, while others say they provide necessary employment

Crofting has been a way of life for generations for many thousands in the Highlands and islands

The people of St Kilda with
the sea birds on which their
fragile economy depended

The men of St Kilda
pictured shortly before the
islands were abandoned

people in what was seen by Victorians as a primitive society. But a combination of disease brought in by tourists and the islanders' own wish to depart to take advantage of a better life elsewhere saw the population decline to under 100 by the First World War. Finally, in the 1920s, illness and emigration halved the population from 73 to 37, and with little demand for the island's produce from its sheep and sea birds, the economy was unsustainable.

St Kilda's depopulation was a peculiar microcosm of what happened in many rural areas of Scotland. Technological advances have made agriculture a much less labour-intensive industry. At the turn of the century, for instance, there were approximately 200,000 working horses in Scotland, with 10,000 people directly employed in their care. The number of working horses has reduced to virtually nil. In 1901 the proportion of the male population working directly in agriculture was 14 per cent, whereas by 1971 that figure was down to 6 per cent. The population of the Highlands fell by 30 per cent in the same period, and by a much higher figure in certain localities. There are now only around 25,000 people employed in the rural mainstays of agriculture, forestry and fishing, down from a figure of 100,000 just after the Second World War.

At the same time, farming as a profession has become much more scientific and the growth of larger-scale farms and battery farming has seen many traditional farming families, particularly tenant farmers, move into other occupations.

The problems faced by farmers in the second half of the twentieth century have been diverse. Britain's entry into the EEC in the 1970s brought with it the Common Agricultural Policy, which has been a boon to some and a hindrance to others. Then, in the last years of the century, two hammer blows struck the industry, and rural Scotland has still not recovered from either.

First, in April 1986, the nuclear power station at Chernobyl near Kiev exploded, and the prevailing winds blew a contaminated cloud of radioactivity over Scotland and other parts of Western Europe. Fears over contamination of the uplands led to hill farmers being prevented from selling their lambs. The hill sheep-farming industry was devastated. Second, the BSE crisis of the last decade proved even more devastating to agriculture as a whole. Although it was argued that Scottish beef farmers should not suffer as badly as their English counterparts since their herds were not so dependent on the contaminated feed which caused the outbreak, nevertheless Scottish cattle had to join the UK-wide cull. It will hopefully not be too many years before the high reputation of Scotch beef is fully restored.

The fishing industry was once one of the largest employers in Scotland, and the herring fleet in particular supported many communities, with work for

Some emigrants went very far from home – this Argentinian gaucho is a native of Lewis

Sheep wait to be sheared at a farmers' competition

One of the sights tourists don't want to see in the Highlands . . .   . . . and one of the views they would like to see

both men and women. Again, technological advances have reduced the labour requirements of fishing – and the industry has faced an even greater threat. Overfishing of the North Sea in particular has led to the virtual destruction of stocks of some species. Cod, haddock and herring fishing are now banned in some sea areas, while in others the European Union's fishing policies restrict catches to hugely unpopular quotas. Fishermen have been paid to scrap their boats and many trawlers lie tied up at anchor. But this is not a new phenomenon – the collapse of the East European export market after the First World War produced the first, and some say the most devastating, crisis in fishing.

Perhaps ironically, the one industry which has offered apparently genuine prospects for rural areas is fish farming. Farmed Scottish salmon is now rural Scotland's most vital export, but again the industry has been hit by fears over disease.

The vagaries of export markets and increased competition from abroad have meant that areas like the Borders have suffered a reduction in demand for locally produced items like wool, once a staple industry across rural Scotland. Many rural industries and crafts now depend on incoming visitors for earnings.

The growth of tourism to Scotland was first encouraged by the railways in

A poster portraying the delights of train travel in Scotland

The train opened up the Highlands to many tourists

Scottish cattle – now free of BSE

Salmon netting, another rural industry under threat

Victorian times, and improved transport and the growth of mass travel have seen tourism become Scotland's largest industry in terms of numbers employed. Tourism has been a boon to many parts of the Highlands in particular, but the immense increase in the number of people visiting rural areas has not been without its problems, especially after the Beeching reforms of the 1960s greatly reduced rural rail services. There is also the problem of land erosion as visitors tramp into the surrounding hills.

In many respects, rural Scotland remains a distinct entity, and although the separate culture of many rural areas has been eroded, there is still a resistance to the complete extinction of such treasures as the Gaelic language, while fundamentalist Christianity is still the dominant cultural force in many parts of the Hebrides.

The continuation of Gaelic has become a symbol of the preservation of rural Scotland. Largely due to migration, the number of Gaelic speakers in Scotland has declined from around 250,000 at the turn of the century to around 60,000 today. But Gaelic as a language was in decline in Victorian times and An Comunn Gaidhealach was founded in 1891 in what was seen even then as a bid to preserve the culture of the Gael. Many would say that the annual Mod has been the greatest achievement of An Comunn, as it provides a focus each year for speakers of the language to meet. The recent establishment of a fund for Gaelic television and films and the publication of Gaelic fiction and poetry have also been hugely important in preserving and encouraging the language. Somhairle MacGill-Eain (Sorley MacLean) was the best-known of the Gaelic poets, but others such as Iain Mac A'Ghobhainn (Iain Crichton Smith), Ruaraidh MacThómais, Domhnall MacAmlaigh (Donald MacAulay), Aonghas MacNeacail and Catriona NicGumaraid have contributed to the preservation and revival of their language.

The arrival of the Scottish Parliament has given hope to many who feel that a legislature closer to home may give Scottish rural issues a higher profile. The fact that the Parliament's signage is written in both languages also encourages many to believe that Gaelic has a brighter future.

THE PROFESSIONS

The three great traditional professions in Scotland are the law, education and medicine. In all three, Scotland retained its sovereignty, so to speak, after the Act of Union in 1707, and Scots are rightly proud of the nation's unique contribution in all of these fields. In the twentieth century, all three professions have undergone considerable upheaval, and though integrated into a wider British and European scene they survive as distinctly Scottish. All three, and particularly health and medicine, are set to take on a new lease of life as they are among the principal responsibilities of the Scottish Parliament.

JUSTICE AND THE LAW

The independence of Scots law was one of the chief guarantees made in the Act of Union, and to this day any threat of erosion of the Scottish legal system is stoutly resisted by Scottish lawyers and politicians. Although the statute book has been vastly changed by Parliament, judges have also made important changes to the law in their judgements.

Like every country, Scotland has had its share of notorious criminal cases in the twentieth century. The most recent mass murderer was Thomas Hamilton at Dunblane, but he never stood trial. In 1958, convicted murderer Peter Manuel not only went to court but conducted his own defence in the latter stages of what was described as the trial of the century. He was eventually convicted of seven murders carried out over two years, though he may have committed up to five more, and he was hanged on 11 July 1958 at Barlinnie prison. The worst Scottish mass murderer of the century was Dennis Andrew Nilsen, a loner who preyed on young men in London. He was finally caught in 1983 when human remains blocked a sewage pipe at his home, ending a five-year killing spree in which he murdered at least 16 men.

A traditional Scottish legal wig

Scots law has prided itself on the avoidance of miscarriages of justice, though this confidence may have been misplaced at times. Only in 1999 did the Scottish Criminal Cases Review Commission begin its work of looking into cases where there remains doubt about convictions; it already has a long waiting list for examination.

The two most notorious miscarriage cases were those of Oscar Slater and Paddy Meehan. Slater was convicted of the December 1908 murder of Miss Marion Gilchrist, but there were doubts in the highest places about the quality of the evidence and the judge's direction to the jury. To the amazement of the press and the public, Secretary of State Lord Pentland commuted the sentence to life imprisonment. The case is said to have directly led to the establishment of the Court of Criminal Appeal, and in 1928, after a long campaign involving Sir Arthur Conan Doyle among others, the Appeal Court freed Slater.

Another famous figure, Ludovic Kennedy, was involved in the long campaign to free Paddy Meehan, a small-time Glasgow criminal who was convicted of murder during a break-in at Ayr.

Peter Manuel being taken into court

Paddy Meehan after his release

Meehan's sensational case included dark hints about secret-service involvement, but his innocence was only finally established after another Glasgow criminal, William Tank McGuinness, was killed, allowing his solicitor, Joseph Beltrami, to reveal the truth of McGuinness's involvement in the first murder.

The longest-running campaign to overturn a verdict is that of Thomas T.C. Campbell and Joseph Steele, convicted in 1984 of Glasgow's worst mass murder of the century in which six members of the Doyle family were burned to death at the end of the so-called ice-cream wars. Campbell and Steele have exhausted the old appeals system and their case is now before the new Review Commission.

The civil law of Scotland has, on occasion, produced cases which have had a worldwide effect. In 1932, a Mrs Donaghue of

Joseph Steele and Thomas
Campbell maintain their
innocence

Paisley unfortunately drank the remains of a decomposing snail in a bottle of ginger beer and became ill. She sued the manufacturer and the case went to the House of Lords before she won a landmark victory which established the extent of a maker's 'duty of care', the judgement later being quoted in many countries.

Reform of Scots law has often been painfully slow, but the establishment of the Scottish Law Commission in 1965 has assisted the process of review. Scots law has on occasion, however, led the world in some fields, notably family law. The Social Work (Scotland) Act of 1968 established Children's Panels which have since been copied in other countries, while Scotland's more liberal approach to licensing law has since been copied in England. Other important reforms included the Conveyancing Act of 1924, the legal aid legislation of 1949 and the land reform acts of 1970 and 1974 which signalled the end of the feudal system, something which should finally be accomplished by the Scottish Parliament in the near future.

The advent of the Scottish Parliament brought with it many huge changes whose ramifications are still not clear. For instance, the European Convention of Human Rights is now part of Scots law and already there have been huge problems for the courts. The Scottish Executive has established a new justice ministry pledging to bring further reforms, and one effect of that was seen in October 1999 when the first-ever advertisement for a Sheriff's post was seen in newspapers. It seems certain that the hitherto secretive system for appointing judges and sheriffs will soon be scrapped and many people have already called for a new and open judiciary appointments system.

The independence of the judiciary, however, will not be compromised. Judges and sheriffs have often used their independence to tackle what they see as injustice; even in the 1990s, the long-running alleged child-abuse case in Orkney hinged on a decision by Sheriff David Kelbie to go against social-work advice.

The profession of the lawyer has also changed considerably in the twentieth century. Until 1949 and the establishment of the Law Society of Scotland, solicitors had little in the way of an organised regulatory system, while the Faculty of Advocates was almost a closed shop jealously preserving its right of appearance before the supreme courts.

The legal profession has extended into many areas of life, particularly into commerce, and the largest property-dealing agencies are now solicitors' property centres. The profession had also opened up to both genders and all social classes, but it wasn't until October 1992 that Scotland's first woman judge, Lady Hazel Aronson, was appointed to the bench.

MEDICINE

Arguably the greatest moment in modern Scottish medicine did not actually take place in Scotland and its significance was not recognised at first. Alexander Fleming was working in his laboratory in St Mary's, Paddington, on a summer's day in 1928 when he noticed that a culture of bacteria had been destroyed by a mould he identified as *Penicillium notatum*. It took 15 years for Oxford scientists led by Howard Florey and Ernst Chain to develop a commercial manufacturing process for penicillin, for which all three were jointly awarded the Nobel prize for medicine in 1945. Fleming never took vast financial reward but was knighted, and by the time he died in 1955 he had the satisfaction of knowing his discovery had already saved thousands of lives.

Other Scottish medical Nobel laureates of the twentieth century included Professor John Macleod, joint winner with Frederick Banting in 1923 for their work in Canada which led to insulin treatment for diabetics. In 1949, Lord John Boyd Orr won the Nobel peace prize for his contribution to the improvement of nutrition across the world. Born in Kilmaurs, Ayrshire, he attended Glasgow University and fought with valour in the First World War, winning the Military Cross and Distinguished Service Order. His research in Scotland led to the conclusion that poverty and malnutrition went hand in hand, and he pioneered free school milk for children as well as helping to devise the wartime diet which meant that, despite rationing, many Britons were actually healthier at the end of the war than they had been in the 1930s. He became the first director of the United Nations Food and Agriculture Organisation.

Nobel laureate Lord Boyd Orr, centre

In 1988, Professor Sir James Black was awarded the Nobel prize for medicine for his discoveries that led to a whole range of everyday drugs such as beta blockers for heart and ulcer patients. Like many great Scottish doctors, he was an unsung hero in his own land. It was only many years after their pioneering work in Edinburgh in the 1950s that full tributes were paid to the team led by Sir John Crofton which developed an effective treatment for tuberculosis, one of the century's biggest killers and, sadly, on the upsurge again around the world.

Although the medical profession has always enjoyed respect in Scotland, the nation as a whole has often been tellingly described as the sick man (and woman) of Europe. At the very start of the century, overcrowding and grossly insanitary conditions in Glasgow led to the last British outbreak of a mediaeval curse. Bubonic plague – the Black Death of centuries before – affected areas of central Glasgow in August and September 1900. At the same time, doctors were trying to contain an out-

break of smallpox around the country. Such diseases as measles, diptheria, polio, whooping cough, croup and scarlatina meant that child mortality in the early part of the century was at a rate we would now consider horrific – on average, 15 per cent of children across Scotland died before the age of five. In addition, life expectancy was less than 50 for men.

Medical advances, some of them pioneered in Scotland, coupled with better housing and environmental health have seen great improvement in these indicators of health. There have on occasion, however, been outbreaks of disease which many people thought had been eradicated. In April 1964, an outbreak of typhoid in Aberdeen led to near panic. The city's schools were closed, children were placed in isolation wards and Aberdeen was effectively placed in quarantine before the problem was brought under control.

For most people, the greatest advance in medicine in the twentieth century was the foundation in 1948 of the National Health Service. Its birth was highly controversial; many doctors and the British Medical Association fiercely opposed the plan at first, but in a national ballot the nation's doctors voted to accept the new service after they were assured they would not become state employees. For the first time, everyone had access to free medical, dental and optical treatment, and although prescription charges later eroded the free aspect of the NHS and various governments have tried to reform the service, the cost of most treatment is still borne by the state rather than the individual.

A Scottish medical degree is still among the most prized in the world, and Scottish medicine is at the forefront in many fields of research. Accompanying medical developments has been the growing biotechnology industry, of which the

The typhoid outbreak in Aberdeen in 1964 saw children placed in isolation wards . . .

. . . while anxious parents crowded round to see them

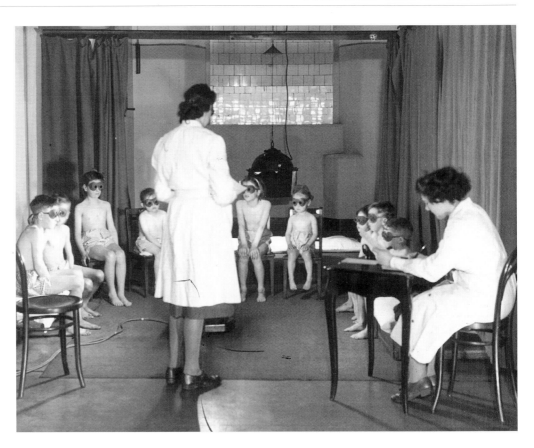

Artificial 'sunshine' was an
early treatment for rickets

Say Hello, Dolly

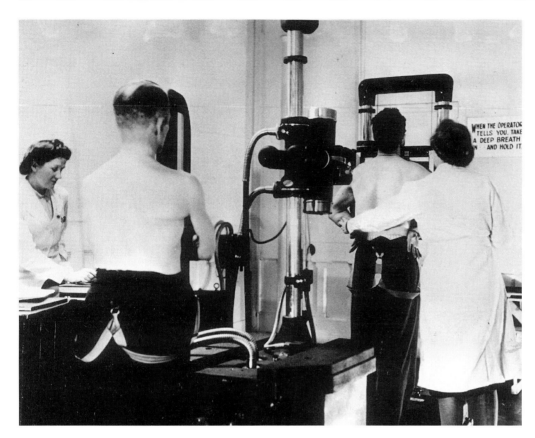

Mass X-ray screening in the 1950s helped defeat tuberculosis

most famous product was Dolly the sheep, the world's first mammal cloned from an adult cell. Dolly's cloning catapulted Scottish biotechnology into the world's headlines and even led to debates in Parliament and the US Congress.

Other medical expertise has been developed in Scotland because of necessity. The successful eradication of the child-crippling disease rickets and mass X-ray screening for tuberculosis were both pioneered in Scotland because of the high incidence of those diseases. Scotland is also home to some of the world's leading heart disease and cancer specialists, reflecting the fact that it has some of the world's highest death rates for these illnesses.

In the 1990s, Scotland has faced new problems which have challenged the medical profession. Many areas of healthcare, including environmental health and bacteriology, came under scrutiny because of an outbreak of E-coli food poisoning emanating from the butcher's shop of John Barr in Wishaw in 1996. The contamination of meat dishes eventually led to the deaths of 22 people, making it the world's worst single outbreak of food poisoning. Scottish research into E-coli is now recognised as world-leading, as is the research into Creuzfeld-Jakob's Disease, the human form of BSE. It was Scottish-based research which first established the link between BSE and CJD and which overturned the government's official position, stated as long ago as May 1990, which was that BSE posed no risk to humans. The UK's CJD surveillance unit is now based at the Western General Hospital in Edinburgh.

The capital also has unrivalled, though unwanted, expertise in dealing with

Butcher John Barr

Samples being taken from
Barr's shop for examination

HIV and AIDS. Edinburgh's drugs underworld was the main conduit for the
rapid spread of HIV in the 1980s, which made the city at one time the AIDS capital of Europe. Pioneering activities such as the establishment of needle-exchange
programmes and improved education about HIV have helped to ensure that the
infection rates did not reach the predicted numbers.

Although spending on health is greater than ever before, many would argue
that the NHS's finances have not kept pace with demand. Healthcare of every
kind was one of the major powers devolved to the Scottish Parliament in 1999,
and the Scottish Executive has already pledged to devote resources to tackling the
nation's ill health.

EDUCATION

Scotland's educational tradition dates back, some say, to John Knox and the Reformers, who, when they effectively governed Scotland in the sixteenth century, insisted on 'a school in every parish'. In fact, King James IV's Education Act in 1496 had already made schooling compulsory for the sons of freeholders, and it is the great Education Act and related acts of this century which have ensured that Scottish education has progressed – though many argue about how far this important sector of Scottish society has actually developed. Free primary education was already in place when the 1908 legislation ensured that schools had the right not just to teach but also to clothe and inspect children's health, and it also guaranteed a certain number of hours of schooling per day.

The 1918 Education Act was a watershed in Scottish society as a whole, not just the world of education. For the first time, religious denominations could insist on publicly funded schools of their own, and the Catholic population duly did so, creating the separate Catholic schools which emphasise Catholic morality but which are, nevertheless, open to all denominations.

The 1918 Act's biggest change was to make free secondary education available to all up to the age of 15, though it took many years for the full implementation of the Act due to the financial crises of the '20s and '30s. Coincidentally,

Scotland introduced compulsory primary and secondary schooling years before most other European countries

Girls learn what we now call home economics at Tynecastle High School in 1913

The only excuse for not paying attention to the teacher – when the photographer came to call

the raising of the school leaving age to 16 was also postponed because of government budget problems and did not take effect until 1973. That change was made by the Labour government of 1964–70 which also introduced comprehensive education, a much more popular policy in Scotland than in England. Within a short period of time, 98 per cent of all Scottish children of secondary-school age were attending comprehensives. The vast majority continue to do so, though there is a small private sector, mainly based on English-type public schools, which has survived from Victorian times to the present day.

For most people under pension age, the biggest single change in education was the introduction of the O Grade examinations in 1962, which replaced previous leaving certificates and which in turn have been replaced by Standard Grades as part of a parcel of reforms introduced by the Conservative government of 1979–97 which also included parental choice of schools and the national curriculum.

The biggest change in the provision of education has been in further education, where the original four universities have been joined by many new universities, many of them converted from colleges of further education in the 1990s. Government figures show that almost 50 per cent of pupils – about 30,000 per year – now go on to some kind of further education. In 1900, by contrast, there were just 6,500 students in further education in Scotland, and university attendance was the exception rather than the rule. Almost all of this expansion took place after the Second World War, and a large proportion of the increase in the number of further education students is due to women's equality.

Education is now the responsibility of the Scottish Parliament, and it is no accident that the first real crisis facing the new government of Scotland is the vexed question of tuition fees. Access to education, it seems, is much more important at the end of the twentieth century than it was at the beginning.

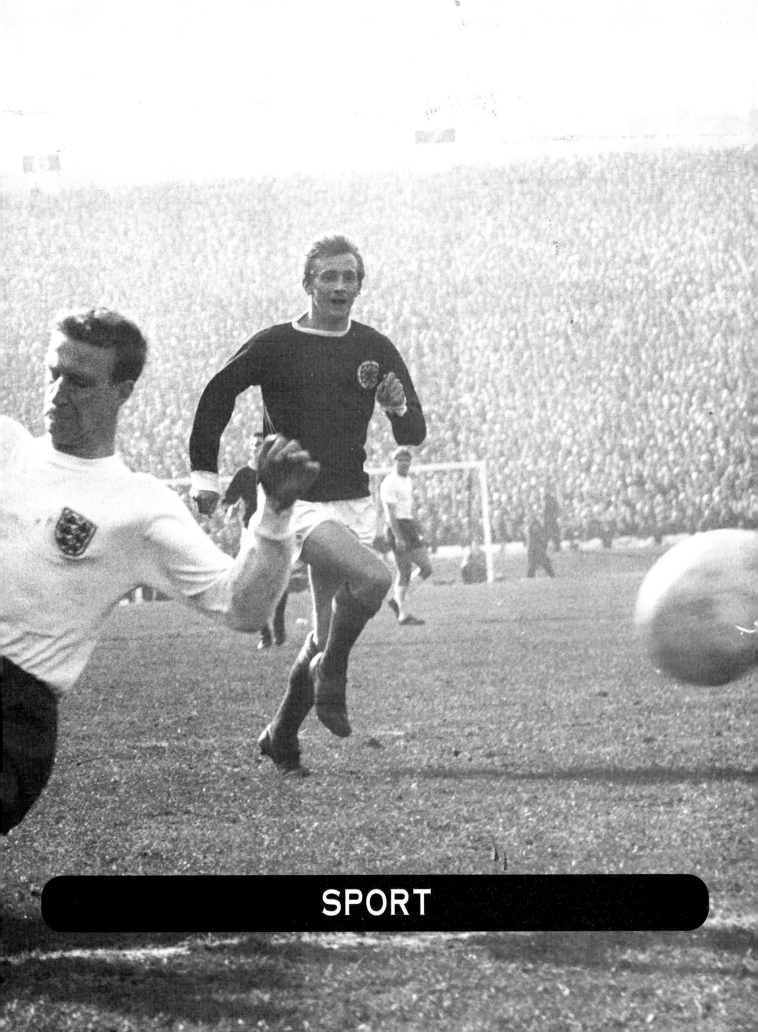

SPORT

Jocky Wilson, darts
champion of the world

Cricket fans show their
allegiance during the 1999
World Cup

The following sporting record of the century concentrates on events that happened in Scotland or which featured Scottish individuals in major performances. Although pride of place is given to six main sports, Scotland has produced many other fine sportsmen and women over the century in sports such as curling, bowls, badminton, rowing and hockey. In cricket – not always thought to be a Scottish game, even though it is our second-largest summer sport after golf – there have been great Scottish players who have had to ply their trade south of the border and represent England. Douglas Jardine, born in India of Scottish parents, captained England in the infamous 'bodyline' tour of Australia in the '30s and, more recently, Mike Denness was a fine captain of Essex and England in the '70s. In 1999, Scotland's cricket team for once captured the imagination of the public by qualifying for the World Cup. Unfortunately, they emulated the football team by going out in the first phase. Scotland's star player, Gavin Hamilton, has since 'graduated' to the full English Test squad.

Individual successes in other sports include such diverse world champions as Jocky Wilson in darts, Peter Haining in rowing's individual sculls and Peter Nicol in squash, while Richard Corsie's four televised World Indoor Bowls championships made the Edinburgh postman a household name. David Wilkie's Olympic 200m breaststroke gold medal in Montreal in 1976 remains the greatest achievement in swimming.

For the most sustained dominance of any sport by a Scot, however, there is

Curling as it was meant to be played – a miniature bonspiel in 1903

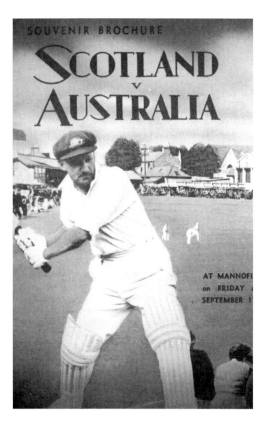

nothing to equal Stephen Hendry's record of seven world snooker titles, the latest achieved in 1999 when many thought his career was over, as he had already been supplanted as world champion and world number one by fellow Scot John Higgins.

A lack of facilities and opportunities has also bedevilled Scottish sport. In racing, for example, Scotland has produced many fine jockeys, especially former champion Willie Carson, but the best have always gone south and only one Scottish horse has been good enough to win a Classic. In May 1962, Rockavon, trained by George Boyd at Dunbar, won the 2,000 Guineas at 66–1. Our National Hunt record is slightly better, but the only Scottish-trained horse to win the Grand National was Rubstic in 1979.

Although many worry about Scotland's sporting future, changes in sports administration and training such as the founding of an Institute of Sport and the promised football academies should mean that in the twenty-first century, as in the twentieth, there will be plenty to cheer about.

A sign of the past – or things to come?

Stephen Hendry, arguably the world's greatest-ever snooker player

Willie Carson, Scotland's finest jockey of all time

David Wilkie shortly after winning his 200m breaststroke Olympic gold medal in a world-record time at Montreal in 1976

Hampden Park shortly after it was built by Archibald Leitch

FOOTBALL

When all else failed, when everything seemed bleak for humanity in the twentieth century, there was one talisman to which Scots could cling to remind them that there was beauty in the world, one method of expression in which Scots were more articulate than most but in which they invested perhaps too much of their national stock of emotion: football.

Often the national sport has become the national obsession, yet football has also been responsible in many instances for engendering a community spirit in an increasingly individualistic society. Great players also have the ability to transport spectators away from the mundane, and Scotland has had its fair share in the twentieth century, Patsy Gallacher, Willie Woodburn, Jim Baxter, Denis Law, Billy Bremner and Kenny Dalglish to name but a few.

The national team has also consistently punched above its true weight and has occasionally caused Scottish chests to burst with pride, never more so than when qualifying for the World Cup in courageous circumstances or when beating the Auld Enemy at Wembley. That they often deflate Scottish spirits by losing to even smaller minnows than themselves is now taken for granted by the Tartan Army, itself the proof that football can be a force for good relations.

The activities of the Old Firm have dominated the country's principal sport. Leaving aside the arguments as to the perhaps dubious nature of how they reached their joint pre-eminence, there can be no denying their superiority on the pitch. In only 15 years of the last 100 has the top league title gone anywhere other than Ibrox or Celtic Park, including a period between 1904 and 1947 when only one other team won the league (Motherwell in 1931–32). Between them they have also won two-thirds of Scottish Cup competitions since 1900, a staggering statistic for a knockout tournament in which, contrary to legend, they have actually played each other many times other than in the final. And in the last years of the century it appears that the clubs themselves have taken the necessary steps to combat the bigotry which has for so long afflicted them.

1902

First Ibrox Disaster

The century of football began badly with the first Ibrox disaster (see report on page 8), after which Ibrox, Celtic Park and Hampden were all redesigned to the formula of a Glaswegian engineer Archibald Leitch, who went on to design many of Britain's greatest stadia.

1904–05

Third Lanark

Formed from a Volunteer Rifle Reserve regiment and founder members of the Scottish Football Association, Third Lanark won the Scottish League in 1904 and the following year won the Cup, briefly threatening to break the emerging stranglehold of the Old Firm.

The Third Lanark team of the early 1900s

1905–10

In 1905, Celtic won the first of a then world record six league titles in a row. In 1907 they became the first club to do the 'double' of league and cup. In 1909, however, came the first real sign of the trouble which the Old Firm could engender. A riot broke out after both the Scottish Cup final and a replay ended in a draw. For the first and only time, the SFA withheld the cup.

Many Scottish teams gave of their best to the war, and some never returned

1914–18

Although the league continued in truncated form, the Scottish Cup was left on the shelf. Many teams lost players in the war – half of the players on Hearts' books were killed or wounded in action – and in most stadia memorial plaques to the clubs' war dead can still be found.

1920s

The period 1920–31 saw the emergence of Rangers as the dominant force in Scottish football, the Ibrox side taking ten titles to Celtic's two. Under the autocratic manager Bill Struth, they developed a direct and vigorous style of team play against which great Celtic individuals such as British record goalscorer Jimmy McGrorry could not compete. Kilmarnock broke the stranglehold, however, with the 1929 Cup final.

Celtic's Jimmy McGrorry heading the goal which gave him the British goalscoring record

Kilmarnock fans on their way to the Scottish Cup final of 1929

31 March 1928

Perhaps the most famous Scottish international team of them all took the field against England at Wembley, where the national team has always been fanatically supported. That day a legend was born as the Wembley Wizards won 5–1, still Scotland's biggest victory over the Auld Enemy.

The immediate pre-war period saw crowds of extraordinary proportions flock to grounds and Hampden in particular, as football became the overwhelming recreational pursuit of the era. The 1937 Scotland v. England international saw a then world record attendance of 149,715, still a European record today. Eight days later, a comparatively light figure of 147,365 people crammed into Hampden for the Celtic v. Aberdeen Scottish Cup final; the attendance remains the European record for a club match. Nor was Old Firm dominance unbroken. In 1938, East Fife became the first and only club from outside the top league to win the Scottish Cup.

After the war came several seasons when the Edinburgh teams were in charge. Hibernian's Famous Five of Bobby Johnstone, Gordon Smith, Lawrie Reilly,

Hearts on their way to winning the Scottish Cup of 1956

Eddie Turnbull and Willie Ormond set new standards for forward play, winning the league three years out of five from 1948 to 1952. The Easter Road side went on to take part in the inaugural European Cup and were only defeated at the semi-final stage in 1955–56.

In 1956 Hearts won the Scottish Cup and became the major force in Scottish football with their own majestic threesome of Conn, Bauld and Wardhaugh. The Tynecastle men went on to win the league twice in three seasons.

The Scotland team of 1957, most of whom later went on to be humiliated at the hands of Paraguay

1958

Having been humiliated 7–0 by Uruguay in the 1954 World Cup finals, in the finals in Sweden Scotland were beaten 3–2 by the unknown team from Paraguay and again went out at the first phase.

25 May 1967

In 1965, a burly ex-miner with a dodgy knee and an indomitable will arrived to manage Celtic after success with Hibs and Dunfermline. Jock Stein was not in the top rank as a player, but as a manager he was second to none. He transformed the Glasgow club into world beaters playing a style of 'total' attacking football. In 1965–66 Celtic won the first of their nine titles in a row, giving them entry to the European Cup for the first time. Some English commentators laughed at Stein when he said Celtic would win the Cup, but on a balmy evening in Lisbon the smiles were all Scottish. Celtic had won every competition they entered that sea-

Celtic's fans acclaim the European Cup
winners of 1967

The Stadium of Light in Lisbon became a sea
of green and white

The biggest upset in Scottish football history – Berwick Rangers defeated Rangers 1–0 in the first round of the Scottish Cup in 1967. Later that year Rangers, Glasgow variety, reached the final of the European Cup-Winners' Cup for the second time in six years. So how good did that make Berwick?

Jimmy Johnstone evades Jack Charlton's tackle in a typical tussle with the Auld Enemy

son and on an unforgettable night 11 men all born within 30 miles of Glasgow destroyed the dire defensive play of Inter Milan for a 2–1 victory. Celtic were the first British – indeed, the first non-Latin – team to win the Cup. It is still the greatest single achievement by a Scottish club.

January 1967

Berwick Rangers beat Rangers 1–0 in the first round of the Scottish Cup, the greatest shock result in Scottish football history.

1967

Jim Baxter and his colleagues toyed with the newly crowned world champions at Wembley. Scotland 'hammered' England 3–2, a result which clearly made them the world's best – at least, that was the fans' theory.

24 May 1972

Rangers became the first Scottish club to win the European Cup-Winners' Cup when they beat Moscow Dynamo 3–2 in Barcelona. Spanish police overreacted to Rangers fans' celebrations and a riot ensued, the infamous Battle of Barcelona leading to Rangers being suspended from the following year's competition. The trouble sadly overshadowed the achievement of what was an excellent team led by the greatest Ranger of them all, John Greig.

John Greig, the greatest Ranger of them all

Wembley, 1977. Scotland
won, the goalposts nil

1974

It had been 16 years since Scotland had qualified for the finals of the world's
greatest tournament and then began a run of qualification which lasted until
France '98 with only the USA in '94 seeing Scotland absent. West Germany '74
saw the team adopt what became a familiar 'gallant losers' mode; even though
unbeaten, Willie Ormond's squad went out on goal difference. Four years later,
led by super-enthusiast Ally McLeod, Scotland went to the World Cup finals in
Argentina as potential world-beaters and came home in sorrow. The greatest
exhibition of Scottish hubris since Flodden Field saw débâcles against 'easy' Iran
and Peru before a brilliant yet ultimately pointless performance against eventual
finalists Holland.

1980s

For a period in the 1980s the 'New Firm' of Aberdeen and Dundee United between them won the title three years in a row, and the Old Firm looked to be almost redundant when Aberdeen also won the European Cup Winners' Cup in 1983, beating Real Madrid in the final. Their manager was Alex Ferguson, who went on to eclipse arguably even Jock Stein's achievements by leading Manchester United to multiple league and cup wins and, his greatest victory of all, the European Cup of 1999, a feat for which he was knighted.

Aberdeen's efforts in the '80s were soon followed by Dundee United's sterling performances in reaching first the semi-final of the European Cup and then the final of the UEFA Cup, which they lost to IFK Gothenburg but which saw their fans universally praised for their sportsmanship.

10 September 1985

Scotland manager Jock Stein collapsed and died shortly before the end of a qualifying match against Wales in Cardiff. It was, said many fans, too high a price to pay for qualification, and in Mexico the following year Scotland were put out by a brutal Uruguayan team.

Sir Alex Ferguson, freeman of Glasgow and perhaps the greatest Scottish manager of all time

His rival for the title – Jock Stein shows Maurice Johnston how it's done

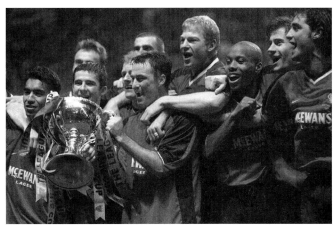

Rangers skipper Terry
Butcher at the start of their
decade of dominance

The latest version of
Scotland's biggest club side

1986–99

New Rangers owner David Murray and manager Graeme Souness started the
Ibrox revolution. They signed Catholics, which the club had not knowingly done
beforehand this century, and imported English and foreign players. Under manager Walter Smith following Souness's departure, Rangers continued to reap rich
dividends. They, too, notched nine-in-a-row league titles and came agonisingly
close to reaching a European Cup final, while their ancient rivals plummeted to
near bankruptcy on a diet of boardroom, managerial and player failure.

1996

In the European Championships in England, Scotland were beaten by the Auld
Enemy at Wembley and again missed out on qualifying for the second phase on
goal difference.

1998 saw World Cup duty for the Tartan Army in France. They were voted
the best supporters in the tournament, but Scotland lost out to Brazil and the
might of Morocco.

The following year the century ended with defeat by England in the Euro 2000
play-off matches.

1997–98

Hearts won the Scottish Cup, while Celtic won the League Cup and the league
under manager Wim Jansen, denying Rangers their much-desired record tenth
title. Jansen resigned days after the title was clinched, provoking huge controversy.

The following season ended in familiar fashion, Rangers winning the Scottish
Cup against Celtic to complete the treble. The Old Firm are now in the top league
of super-rich clubs in Europe and no one else in Scotland can compete, or so it
seems.

See you, Joaquim – the fans of two great footballing nations meet before the opening match of the World Cup in France, 1998

John Collins after he scored from the penalty spot in that game

RUGBY

Scotland's second major team sport is rugby union. For too long rugby was largely the preserve of middle-class private schools, with only the Borders displaying a classless approach to the sport in the true heartland of the game in Scotland.

Scotland has sat at the top table of world rugby since the outset largely because of the sheer weight of tradition, as often there has not been the player base to justify that position. Thankfully, however, Scotland has from time to time produced players and teams capable of beating everybody – New Zealand excepted – and attacking full-backs Ken Scotland, Andy Irvine and Gavin Hastings are among the finest players of the modern era.

1900–38

In what was arguably Scotland's finest decade, the Triple Crown – defeats of England, Ireland and Wales – was achieved in 1901, 1903 and 1907. Then, in 1922, after years of staging internationals at Inverleith, the Scottish Rugby Union announced plans to build a stadium and move its headquarters to a greenfield site at Murrayfield on the west side of Edinburgh. In that year an Edinburgh University student called Eric Liddell won the first of his seven caps for Scotland.

In 1925 Scotland won its first Grand Slam with a team containing the peerless Ian Smith, the winger who still holds the record for the most consecutive tries in a Five Nations Championship, comprising the last three scored against Wales and the first three against France. The Triple Crown was then won in 1933 and 1938.

The 1925 Grand Slam side

As France took no part in the championship in either of those years, Scotland had a 100 per cent international record. But in 1951, the nadir of Scottish rugby came: South Africa won by the unprecedented score of 44–0. It was the start of a decade of failure, though the '60s and '70s saw some revival in Scotland's fortunes.

The Greens of Hawick in their heyday

1973

League rugby was introduced, with Hawick winning the first five titles. They have undoubtedly been the greatest club side over the course of the century.

Beating England at
Murrayfield. Not a recent
picture

1975

With a mighty Welsh team at its peak and Scotland going well, a world record attendance of 104,000 crowded into Murrayfield to see the contest between the two sides. The record stood until 1999, when 107,000 attended the Bledisloe Cup match between Australia and New Zealand in Sydney's new Olympic stadium.

1984

A Scottish team of few stars but invincible togetherness and led by an inspirational captain, Jim Aitken, won the Grand Slam under coach Jim Telfer.

1987

Scotland took part in the first World Cup in 1987, drawing with France and beating Zimbabwe and Romania before losing to eventual winners New Zealand.

Scotland skipper Jim Aitken in triumph at the conclusion of the 1984 Grand Slam victory over France

17 March 1990

Another great coach-and-captain team, Ian McGeechan and David Sole, led Scotland to its greatest-ever achievement. England had swept all before them in the Five Nations and came to Murrayfield as hot favourites for the match where, for the first time, the winners would lift all the prizes available to the home international teams. The Calcutta Cup – presented annually to the winners of the Scotland v. England match – the Triple Crown, the Five Nations Championship and the Grand Slam went to Scotland, who won 13–7 after one of the most intense and passionate rugby matches ever played. England got their revenge the following year, winning the Grand Slam and pipping Scotland in the semi-final of the World Cup. It was still Scotland's best performance in the tournament to date, featuring victories over Ireland, Zimbabwe, Japan and Western Samoa.

Gary Armstrong ignited the move which led to Tony Stanger's clinching try in the winner-takes-all Grand Slam game of 1990

Gavin Hastings on his way
to scoring against France in
Paris in 1995

1995

Following their first victory in Paris since 1968, and after losing the Five Nations by a single defeat against England, Scotland performed creditably in that year's World Cup, beating Tonga and the Ivory Coast but losing to France and New Zealand. However, the advent of professionalism in rugby union in 1995 caught the SRU and, indeed, most national unions unawares, and Scotland went into a brief decline.

1999

Even with coaches Jim Telfer and Ian McGeechan – recognised as among the world's best and chosen to coach the 1997 British Lions – back at the helm, Scotland were 100–1 outsiders for the last Five Nations Championship. Revelling in the role of underdog and playing a new and exciting style of rugby, they won the title before going on to perform well in the fourth World Cup, being put out in the quarter-final by their eternal nemesis New Zealand.

The last Five Nations championship went to Scotland after their dramatic win in Paris and Wales's even more dramatic victory over England in April 1999

The end of two great careers: Scotland coach Jim Telfer comforts a weeping Gary Armstrong after the All Blacks eliminated Scotland from the Rugby World Cup finals in October 1999

ATHLETICS

1924

Having already represented Scotland seven times at rugby, Eric Liddell, arguably Scotland's greatest individual sportsman of the twentieth century, was picked to represent Britain in the Paris Olympics. Son of a missionary family, Liddell's speed on the track was such that he was already a multiple record holder at 100m and 200m. In Paris his Christian beliefs made him refuse to run in heats to be held on a Sunday, but he switched to the 400m, a distance which he was not known for running, and in the final broke the world record to lift the gold medal. He gave up the promise of fame and fortune to become a missionary in China and he died of a brain tumour in a Japanese prisoner-of-war camp in 1945. His fame endures, however, especially after his Olympic feat was portrayed in the Oscar-winning film *Chariots of Fire*.

1970

The Commonwealth Games were held in Edinburgh and were dubbed 'The Friendly Games' thanks to the warmth of participants and spectators alike. Wearing borrowed shoes, Ian Stewart won gold in the 5,000m and Lachie Stewart (no relation) won the 10,000m gold. Scotland's women's team excelled themselves that year too, Rosemary Payne and Rosemary Stirling winning the discus and 800m respectively.

1980

Scotland finally got that 100m gold denied to Liddell. Allan Wells had started life as a long jumper but switched to sprinting and in the Moscow Olympics he took the top prize. The Americans had boycotted those Olympics, but shortly afterwards in Germany Wells beat all their top sprinters to prove his win was a genuine achievement.

Ian Stewart leads Ian McCafferty over the line for a Scottish one-two in the 5,000m at the Commonwealth Games in Edinburgh, 1970

Olympic champion Allan Wells beats his rivals to the line yet again

Opposite: The Flying Scotsman Eric Liddell

Liz McColgan, Scotland's
only athletics world
champion, seen here
winning the gold medal at
the 1986 Commonwealth
Games in Edinburgh

McColgan and her great
rival Yvonne Murray, now
sadly retired

1986

At the Commonwealth Games, just one track medal was won by
Scotland, Liz Lynch – later Liz McColgan – winning the 10,000m
before going on to win over the same distance at the World
Championships. Had McColgan and another European and
Commonwealth champion, Yvonne Murray, stayed clear of
injury, they could have dominated women's distance running in
the 1990s.

GOLF

The major sport universally acknowledged as Scotland's gift to the world is golf, and the twentieth century has seen many fine Scottish players, male and female, lift championships galore. Yet the biggest prize of all, the Open Championship, has eluded great Scottish players such as Eric Brown, Brian Gallacher, Sam Torrance and – so far – Colin Montgomerie, Europe's record money-winner.

ANY PERSONS (EXCEPT PLAYERS) CAUGHT COLLECTING GOLF BALLS ON THIS COURSE WILL BE PROSECUTED AND HAVE THEIR BALLS REMOVED

We think we know what they mean. Sign on a Scottish golf course which shall remain nameless

Golf was arguably Scotland's first unisex sport – Mary, Queen of Scots, enjoyed a round, and putting competitions were great favourites among women in Edwardian times

1901–10

The century started with Scottish dominance of the Open, however. James Braid won five Open titles between 1901 and 1910, and went on to leave his stamp all over golf with his excellence in designing courses.

1931

Acknowledged as a Scot despite having become an American citizen, Tommy Armour won the Open at Carnoustie in 1931.

1970

Scotland has staged some epic Opens, but few compare with Doug Sanders' final-hole drama when he missed a three-foot putt against Jack Nicklaus at St Andrews. Nicklaus, the Golden Bear, remains an idol to Scottish fans and his love of Scottish golf is such that he named his Ohio course after Muirfield.

1977

Perhaps the greatest Open Championship ever took place at Turnberry when Tom Watson, who won all five of his Opens in Scotland, and Jack Nicklaus went head-to-head over two days of supreme golf, the title only being decided on the 72nd green.

Scots-born Tommy Armour, then a US citizen, with the famous claret jug after the 1931 Open at Carnoustie

Doug Sanders ducks as Jack Nicklaus throws his club aloft upon winning their famous duel at St Andrews in 1970

An even more famous duel – Nicklaus beaten by Tom Watson at Turnberry in 1977

1985

Sandy Lyle became the first Scot to win the Open for 54 years at Sandwich. The following year he won the US Masters, becoming the first British golfer to claim that coveted title. The year also saw the high point of Sam Torrance's career, when he struck the winning putt to lift the Ryder Cup for Europe.

1999

Paul Lawrie from near Aberdeen won the Open at Carnoustie in sensational fashion following a play-off to become the first home-based Scot to win the Open on Scottish soil since Braid's 1910 victory at St Andrews. Lawrie was dismissed as lucky by many a commentator because the French golfer Jean Van der Velde threw away the title with bizarre play on the last hole, but Lawrie duly became the joint top individual scorer at the infamous Ryder Cup battle at Brookline, Massachusetts.

Two of the great figures of Scottish golf: Ryder Cup captain Bernard Gallacher and Open and Masters champion Sandy Lyle

The 1999 Open champion Paul Lawrie sinks the winning putt at Carnoustie

BOXING

Boxing has seen great Scottish individual champions, most of whom, it must be said, were diminutive in stature. No Scot has ever won or even competed for the world heavyweight championship, but Scotland has had seven world champions at lighter weights during the twentieth century.

1935

Benny Lynch was the first world champion, winning the world flyweight title by beating Jackie Brown in Manchester in September 1935, at the age of 22. Overwhelmed by fame, he lost the title by failing to make the weight before his life spiralled into alcoholism and early death at the age of just 33. A premature death was also suffered by Jackie Paterson, who became world flyweight champion in 1943 by beating Peter Kane at Hampden. Paterson, from Springside in Ayrshire, lost his title in 1948 to Rinty Monaghan and then emigrated. He was killed in South Africa in 1966 at the age of 46.

Benny Lynch in the far corner after his world-title fight in 1935

Dick McTaggart (right), Scotland's only Olympic boxing gold medallist

1956

Scotland's greatest amateur boxer Dick McTaggart, later a respected coach, won gold at the Melbourne Olympics and was voted the best boxer of the Games.

1966

Walter McGowan of Burnbank near Hamilton won the world flyweight championship from Salvatore Burruni at Wembley, before losing it two years later to Chartchai Chinoi.

World champion Jim Watt leads the crowd in a chorus of 'Flower of Scotland'

The man reckoned by most experts to be Scotland's finest boxer, Ken Buchanan of Edinburgh, won the world lightweight title in September 1970, beating Ismael Laguna in San Juan. In the eyes of most onlookers he was robbed of the title two years later, when Roberto Duran hit the Scot with a low blow which the referee mysteriously ignored.

Jim Watt was perhaps Scotland's most popular champion, his lightweight title being won against Colombian Alfredo Pitalua in April 1979. He defended his title four times, including a superb performance against American Howard Davis at Ibrox Park, before defeat by Alexis Arguello caused him to retire in 1981, after which he became a successful boxing commentator.

Pat Clinton and Paul Weir are Scotland's latest champions, Clinton winning the world flyweight championship before Weir became the first Scot to win world titles at different weights, clinching the straw-weight title in 1993 and the light-fly title the following year.

MOTOR RACING

Scotland has produced some of the world's finest racing drivers, from the Ecurie Ecosse team in their saltire-blue Jaguars to David Coulthard in Formula One in 1999. In rallying, too, Scotland has had a world champion and a notable 'first family'.

1901

A car built by Albion Motors in Glasgow came second in the 500-mile trial held by the Royal Automobile Club. The first Scottish International Rally was held in 1932, 27 years after the Royal Scottish Automobile Club held its first trials.

An early hill-climb, forerunner to the Scottish Rally

A rare picture together of Scotland's two world champion motor racing drivers, Jackie Stewart and Jim Clark (right)

1956

Against expectations, the Ecurie Ecosse team won the Le Mans 24-hour race and repeated the feat the following year, before one of the Ecurie Ecosse graduates, Innes Ireland, became the first Scot to win a Grand Prix in America in 1961.

1962–68

Jim Clark, ranked by many alongside Brazilian Ayrton Senna as the greatest natural driving talent the world has ever seen, dominated Grand Prix racing in the 1960s, winning 25 races and twice winning the world championship, becoming the first Scot to win the title in 1963. Born in Fife and raised in the Borders, Clark was both handsome and charming, and his death in an accident at Hockenheim in 1968 caused great mourning across Scotland. Following in his footsteps and eventually even beating Clark's record, Dumbarton-born Jackie Stewart survived a serious accident to become Scotland's greatest racing champion. He clinched the 1969 Formula One title with an exciting victory in Italy and won the world title three times before retiring in 1973. The lure of the track was irresistible,

Colin McRae on his way to winning the World Rallying Championship

however, and after becoming a multi-millionaire businessman, Stewart set up a Formula One team in 1996 with his son Paul.

1995

Colin McRae became the first Scot to win the World Rallying Championship. His father Jimmy won five British Open Rally Championships and his brother Alistair is also a top rally driver.

A McRae family portrait

1999

Just three years after starting up, the Stewart team won the European Grand Prix, having been sold to Ford to race under the Jaguar banner. Also in 1999, David Coulthard of Twynholm again demonstrated his potential by winning more Formula One races in a McLaren. He could well be Scotland's next world champion.